PRAISE FOR *WHY CALL IT GOD?*

"In *Why Call it God?*, Rabbi Mecklenburger continues with insightful inquiries into the connections between religion and science. He demonstrates effectively that religious concepts from Judaism and other faith traditions have continued relevance for our daily lives in an age of scientific advancement and skepticism."

—DANIEL S. LEVINE, PROFESSOR OF PSYCHOLOGY, UNIVERSITY OF TEXAS AT ARLINGTON

"In our increasingly secular age, Rabbi Ralph Mecklenburger explores faith and how to think about and speak of God and ourselves in more meaningful ways. ... Mecklenburger makes a persuasive case for 'Order of Being' as language for God reflective of our times and explains why we need to think about this important topic. He reflects, builds upon, and incorporates the tenor of our times in ways that I, as a Roman Catholic, found *tov me'od* (very good) for my *nephesh* (self, soul)."

—TONI CRAVEN, EMERITA PROFESSOR OF HEBREW BIBLE, BRITE DIVINITY SCHOOL AT TEXAS CHRISTIAN UNIVERSITY

"Rabbi Mecklenburger examines the timeless principles of faith in light of twenty-first-century knowledge. Leaving no essential religious question unaddressed, his compelling and thoughtful conclusions will illuminate and animate the life and faith of every reader."

—RICHARD AGLER, RABBI EMERITUS, CONGREGATION B'NAI ISRAEL OF BOCA RATON

"Recognizing that all language for God is metaphorical, Rabbi Mecklenburger shows how the concept that God is a person has become increasingly problematic, leading some persons away from faith. In its place, he offers a philosophical metaphor for God that he argues persuasively will allow persons troubled by the personal metaphor to believe that there is more to life than accident, that beyond life's pleasures, and despite our obvious frailty and inevitable death, our lives do matter; that they have purpose and meaning. Persons acquainted with the Abrahamic faiths—Judaism, Christianity, and Islam—will appreciate Mecklenburger's attention to the relationship of his philosophical metaphor for God to the Hebrew Scriptures and contemporary religious practices."

—D. NEWELL WILLIAMS, PRESIDENT AND PROFESSOR OF MODERN AND AMERICAN CHURCH HISTORY, BRITE DIVINITY SCHOOL AT TEXAS CHRISTIAN UNIVERSITY

"Too often, our language about God is stuck in the past. But just as human beings, culture and even Judaism itself have evolved and changed over time, our views of God need to evolve, as well. Rabbi Mecklenburger and *Why Call It God?* approach some of the most challenging theological topics—from mitzvot to covenant to prophecy—with rationality and a scientific mindset, helping us develop dynamic new ways to think about and talk about God."

—GEOFFREY A. MITELMAN, FOUNDING DIRECTOR, SINAI AND SYNAPSES

Why Call It God?

Why Call It God?

Theology for the Age of Science

RALPH MECKLENBURGER

foreword by Sheldon Zimmerman

WIPF & STOCK · Eugene, Oregon

WHY CALL IT GOD?
Theology for the Age of Science

Wipf & Stock
An Imprint of Wipf and Stock Publishers
199 W. 8th Ave., Suite 3
Eugene, OR 97401

www.wipfandstock.com

PAPERBACK ISBN: 978-1-7252-8493-7
HARDCOVER ISBN: 978-1-7252-8494-4
EBOOK ISBN: 978-1-7252-8495-1

11/20/20

For our grandchildren,
Leah, William, Levi, and Hannah

Contents

Foreword

The author Ralph Mecklenburger confronts the reader with the reality of the critical issues in formulating a theology for the age of science. In earlier times many writers and thinkers have formulated theologies confronting and considering the cultural, intellectual, and religious challenges of their time.

In their creative work and faith traditions they have brought us to new and exciting understandings. Their work has led us over the millennia to creative traditions and insights that have determined our beliefs and understandings of our place in the universe and relationships with each other and reality.

Today more than ever before the increasingly secular nature of Western societies has posed far more intellectual challenges to religion. Ralph Mecklenburger's life as a rabbi, teacher, and humanly sensitive leader of a religious institution has enabled him to understand and respond to the challenges of science while providing new understanding of God and the divine. As he insists for us: "This is a book about God . . . for educated twenty-first-century people." "We need to . . . turn to the image of God as the order or ground of being." "The best metaphor is God as order of being."

Metaphors and myths are the instruments that help us structure reality for ourselves, the history of our world, and what its future should be. We genuinely need these metaphors and myths, not as "fairy tales" but as serious instruments of the searching for faith and the order of being. Professor Sidney Hook in his work *The Metaphysics of the Instrument* helps us understand that our instruments create the realities with which we live, and help us live and create with them. We create and understand the world by the instruments we use. God as the order of being becomes the metaphor for our relationships with each other, the world, and all existence.

Rabbi Mecklenburger reminds us of the work of Maimonides (RAM-BAM) and his doctrine of negative attributes when speaking or thinking about God. "Double negatives" must be used in order to state that they cannot apply to God. Any use of human attributes in speaking of God leads us to make what contemporary philosophers called "category errors." Human attributes cannot be used to describe God in rational terms. As Mecklenburger points out, "faith must not contradict scientific evidence"; "faith is tied up with our sense of meaning in our lives." He sets up the stage for a more abstract and philosophical idea of God.

So what then can we say about God? He labels as "divine intangibles" phenomena that make meaning and purpose possible in our lives, for example, truth, justice, love, beauty, hope, etc. "God must not be thought of as a flesh and blood person, and need not be thought of as a personal, person-like" thing. RAMBAM rejects the idea that God has emotions at all.

Rabbi Mecklenburger reminds us that "Some modern Christian theologians would agree, among them Paul Tillich, who spoke of God as 'the ground of being,' and Charles Hartshorne, who understood God as 'process.'"

Mecklenburger continues to enrich our knowledge and sensitivity to others and the world through his view of God, his study of revelation, the "universal" God, the search for spirituality, the place of rituals, historical, ancient and/or modern, and the place of prophecy. He evaluates the meaning of our loving God, sensing God in worship, and *mitzvah* (the feeling of what is mandated). Morality itself, he teaches, may be better served by philosophical God concepts—philosophically "mandated."

So why call the order of being "God"? This book comes to give us the reason and path for the journey, the hope that our struggles in the world have purpose and meaning, that there is an order, almost messianic in nature, that we need not dismiss the rational in order to give meaning, nor dismiss the traditional rituals in order to be rational and modern. We are taught that through human creativity and our work or power *we* can achieve holiness. He writes that "the Messiah who isn't coming" can be understood as the Messiah who is "justice incarnate." We *can* achieve holiness! There is purpose and meaning in the order of being.

As we read this book a light shines, calling us to new understandings and a life path. We can attain holiness.

SHELDON ZIMMERMAN,
Past President, Central Conference of American Rabbis
Past President, Hebrew Union College—Jewish Institute of Religion

Acknowledgments

I gratefully acknowledge countless professors and colleagues over the years, as well as the wonderful community at Beth-El Congregation in Fort Worth, Texas, who have encouraged my independent thinking for three and a half decades. My wife, Ann, too, there for me for nearly half a century, put up with my nearly obsessive concern to finish these chapters.

In addition, I offer heartfelt thanks for the time, wisdom, and encouragement of four readers of earlier drafts who suggested corrections and clarifications. First, Rabbi Neil Gillman, of blessed memory, professor of Jewish philosophy at the Jewish Theological Seminary of America, left his mark. On summer study leaves I was also made very welcome by the library staff at the New York campus of my rabbinic school *alma mater*, the Hebrew Union College-Jewish Institute of Religion. How nice that an HUC-JIR president, Rabbi Sheldon Zimmerman, with whom I had formed a friendship while he was senior rabbi of Temple Emanu-El in Dallas, moved back to the DFW metroplex a couple of years ago. When I saw him one day and mentioned I was finishing up this book, he generously offered to read it, and made helpful suggestions. I am grateful for his friendship, his enthusiasm for my work, and for the foreword he graciously provided.

There is a seminary in Fort Worth, as well, Brite Divinity School, where I have been welcomed as adjunct faculty many times over the years. At Brite I came to know Dr. Toni Craven, a delightful, insightful, and now emerita professor of Hebrew Bible. Her comments and suggestions improved the two chapters here on "The Mystery of Prophecy." A book involving science needed a critical reading by someone outside the world of theological studies too! My friend and congregant Dr. Howard Kelfer, a pediatric neurologist who shares my enthusiasm for the relatively new field of cognitive studies, again (as with my previous book) read the manuscript and made notes and suggestions.

Responsibility for any errors, of course, rests with me and not these wonderful friends, but their help and encouragement have meant a great deal to me.

Ralph Mecklenburger

Abbreviations

HEBREW BIBLE

Dan	Daniel
Deut	Deuteronomy
Eccl	Ecclesiastes
Exod	Exodus
Ezek	Ezekiel
Gen	Genesis
Isa	Isaiah
Jer	Jeremiah
Judg	Judges
1–2 Kgs	First and Second Kings
Lev	Leviticus
Mal	Malachi
Mic	Micah
Neh	Nehemiah
Num	Numbers
Prov	Proverbs
Ps	Psalms
1–2 Sam	First and Second Samuel
Song	Song of Songs

NEW TESTAMENT

1 Cor	First Corinthians
Eph	Ephesians
Matt	Matthew

RABBINIC LITERATURE

Avot R. Nat.	*Avot de Rabbi Nathan* (Midrash)
b.	Babylonian Talmud
B. Bat.	*Bava Batra* (Talmudic Tractate)
Ber.	*Berakhot* (Talmudic Tractate)
Eccl. Rab.	Ecclesiastes (Qoheleth) *Rabbah*
Eruv.	*Eruvin* (Talmudic Tractate)
Exod. Rab.	*Sh'mot Rabbah*
Gen. Rab.	*Bereshit Rabbah*
Midr. Rab.	*Midrash Rabbah*
m.	Mishnah
Sanh.	*Sanhedrin* (Talmudic Tractate)
Shab.	*Shabbat* (Talmudic Tractate)
Song Rab.	*Shir Hashirim Rabbah*

Introduction

My wife and I and several friends took a vacation cruise recently, and hired a van and guide to show us around when we docked in Lisbon. As we returned to port, our guide, Carlos, took us to a sixteenth-century cathedral which contained the sarcophagus of the famous explorer Vasco da Gama. There were worshipers present, yet the huge sanctuary was far from full. One of our little group asked Carlos if he was Catholic, and he responded, "This is a Catholic country. I got a Catholic education as a child. It's like if you ask me do I have a bicycle? I have a bike. But I don't ride very often." That is contemporary secularism in a nutshell. Religion and its expressions are regarded by many as important aspects of our cultural legacy, but are peripheral to many people's daily lives. Visit Europe or the Middle East and classic cathedrals and synagogues are not to be missed, which does not mean that the same travelers attend worship or study sessions in their home synagogues or churches very often.

Clergy such as I am—a retired rabbi, but I still do my best to help out in my home congregation and to serve small congregations from time to time—do our best to lead worship, and to teach and preach. Most congregations have a saving remnant of "regulars" who show up for weekly Sabbath worship services. Some, no doubt, find spiritual uplift, as well as the comfortable feeling of participating in a community. Others come occasionally, attracted by any number of enticements—an announced sermon topic or musical program, a children's service, family occasion, or whatever else we clergy and our lay committees can come up with. We honor various individuals and groups, such as the third grade in religious school, or women's or men's auxiliary members, with roles in the worship. They come for their honors, or to proudly see their children or grandchildren participating, but are not back the next week simply to pray and enjoy the fellowship. This is not merely the result of members' busy lives, but rather reflects the increasingly secular nature of Western societies (I understand the phenomenon is worse in Europe than America).

With the mercantile mindset of our society, we are apt to think of other religions or denominations as "the competition." Yet the church next door or the synagogue across town are likely also concerned with poor attendance. Our problem is not one another, but growing secularism. Being more creative in worship or more welcoming as religious communities in our anonymous cities, offering better youth groups and religious schools— all the standard methods we keep working at to address the problem—are good. But they only nibble away at the margins. The problem is faith. The problem is our understanding—or *mis*understanding—of God. The foundation of religion is the Divine. If people truly believed God was listening to their prayers and might treat them differently based on their participation, they would attend worship more regularly, think of religion more often at home and work, and employ home rituals to help them sense God's presence in their lives. All the gimmicks in the world will not fill the pews unless we rethink what modern people, in this scientific, technological age, can find theologically compelling and sustaining.

So this is a book about God, or at least my idea of a believable God for educated twenty-first-century people. I wrote a science-and-religion book, *Our Religious Brains*, in which I explained early on that all God talk is metaphorical and inexact because no one fully understands how the universe operates, and the eternal God is utterly different from us mortals. I intentionally did not go too deeply into the topic of God, preferring to stress instead the human side of the encounter with God. The very structure of our brains, and the way they function, help explain why we believe and behave religiously, from faith and spirituality to morality and ritual. There was enough that could be controversial already without my pressing on changing the dominant metaphor for God. Then, as I flew around the country for a while doing book talks, I found lots of people asking good and logical questions . . . about God! So I gradually came to the realization that I needed to write not another predominantly science-and-religion book, but a mostly theological book, albeit enriched here and there by science. I will challenge the reader to consider that God, while real, is not a conscious being hearing your prayers and pulling the strings in "his" world. Important questions then arise. If God is not a conscious "king," what are prophecy and revelation? Why pray? Are holidays and a thousand other religious deeds (for Jews the word is *mitzvot*, "commandments") suddenly optional? How can we "serve" a God who—or really which—does not in any literal way know he—it—is being served?

Before my formal retirement the people of Beth-El Congregation in Fort Worth generously allowed me to go for a month or two each summer on study leaves in New York. Periodically I would take the subway from the sublet apartment Ann and I had rented to the Upper East Side to visit Neil Gillman, of blessed memory, first in his office at the Jewish Theological Seminary of America, where he was professor of Jewish philosophy, and then after he retired and his health was declining, to his apartment. After *Our Religious Brains* came out (with Neil's appreciative preface), one summer I made the usual pilgrimage, this time to share preliminary thoughts for this current book. I was hatching a book about the implications for modern religion of a God conceived of less as personal (person-like: the familiar creator-father-king-judge idea of God) and more as philosophical (not the author of the laws of nature, but the laws themselves; not the giver of meaning, but, so to speak, the meaning itself). As I was talking about the laws of physics, the amazing but blind process of evolution, about truth and compassion, etc., my teacher blurted out, "But why call it God?!"

Gillman was asking me this?! He had studied with Mordecai Kaplan, who spoke of God as a "process making for good." Could he be serious?! "Call it whatever you want!" I countered. "Call it Irving! The question is not what to call it, but is it true?!" He smiled. "That's what Kaplan said," my mentor told me.

I think it was the next summer that I was back, and anxious to share a purple prose paragraph I thought Gilman would love. It asserted that love was no less profound for being itself divine, rather than a conscious gift from the Divine, that nature was no less awe inspiring for having evolved to its current complexity and grandeur than had it been planned by a divine artist . . . and so on and so forth. "Mush," he said. "It sounds like a eulogy any rabbi would give." Eulogy? I was not saying God was dead, merely that we needed to understand God in more abstract ways, albeit ways that could still inspire. He did not mean to imply that I was eulogizing God, he explained, but that from me, after all these years, he expected academic argument, not rhetorical flourish. Back to the drawing board . . .

❖ ❖ ❖

The plan of *Why Call It God?*, then, is fairly straightforward. Chapter 1 offers a diagnosis of the malady afflicting modern Western religion. Even as many sincerely claim that they are proud of their religious heritage, af-filiation with religious institutions, and worship attendance, are down. The clichéd question is hyperbolic but telling: Why are the pews empty? One reason is theological: the problem of how a loving and just God allows mass murder, on the one hand, and on the other hand natural catastrophes from individuals' cancers to massive disasters—earthquakes, hurricanes, volcanic eruptions, and other "acts of God" (as the insurance industry terms them). The problem of evil, we might say, has always been the Achilles' heel of monotheism. With our vaunted modern medicine the death of children may shock us more than ever, and with our amazing communications we are more aware than ever when mass casualties occur. A second reason for religion's decline is the dramatic rise of scientific knowledge in recent centuries, which seems to be picking up speed in recent decades. No longer do people instinctively turn to religion for answers when we want to know where things come from, how they operate, or how we might address problems (faced with a new health threat—COVID-19 most recently—we turn first to medical science, not prayer). Likewise, we look to technology for continued improvements to the quality of life. Technology has also brought us weapons of mass destruction and global warming, of course. Wisely or not, for help with such issues we are more apt to look for further technological innovation than to religion. Science pushing religion aside is but one of many forces behind the third challenge, the growing secularism of our age, which has philosophical and political roots as well.

With some of religion's chief dilemmas thus sketched, chapter 2 turns to the theological approach which I suggest will help us at least sidestep the problem of evil, make our awareness of God compatible with the dominant scientific worldview, and perhaps even begin to open the minds and hearts of secularized moderns to religious experience. We need, however reluctantly, to let go of our image of God as loving friend or leader, and turn to the image of God as the order of being. First we shall speculate about the origins of the misleading personal God metaphors in the process of showing that the forces to which ancients were reacting are no less real and important to moderns. But there are less flawed metaphors available to help us relate to them. To my mind the best metaphor is God as order of being. That includes, but is not limited to, the physical order which science explores. Furthermore, our hunger for meaning and spirituality are tied up with the way we experience the world, which is emotional at least as much as rational. The quintessential religious moment occurs when objective reality and subjective human experience, the presence of order and our apprehension of it, come together. We can notice, and in some ways ourselves create, what I call "divine intangibles." That is a fancy way of affirming the reality and meaningfulness, as part of the fabric of being of which we ourselves are a part, of a host of realities we appreciate without always being able to fully define. Among the divine intangibles are beauty, justice, love, truth, creativity, courage, hope, and more. These are what most of us recognize as the things that make our lives worth living.

While I regard order of being as the best metaphor for God, I hasten to add that my answers to the questions that follow in subsequent chapters may work as well for other philosophical God concepts. Readers may have pondered God as the greatest good of which we can conceive, as process in history, as ground of being, or perhaps have entertained the notion that God is nature or the universe (pantheism, and much mysticism). These ideas of divinity are not necessarily mutually exclusive. Once we recognize that all God talk is approximate and metaphorical, saying as much about our perception of holiness as about holiness itself, we can use multiple metaphors—even human ones. Still, I maintain, the anthropomorphic God concept, expressed with human metaphors such as king, judge, and father, creates unrealistic expectations of divine intervention in the order, and thus disillusionment and doubt.

Subsequent chapters turn to the questions which flow from affirming a philosophical God concept, especially for those accustomed to thinking of God as person-like. Chapters 3 and 4 take up prophecy, which is worthy of the most extended attention because Judaism, Christianity, and Islam are Scripture-based religions which have asserted that God has directly given us words, or at least ideas, recorded by prophets in texts. God would have to be a person-like, "anthropomorphic" being to do that. How could we know, and for that matter how might the prophets themselves have honestly believed, that they were speaking for God? Experienced students of the Hebrew Bible (Tanakh) will not be surprised to find that biblical generations themselves found prophecy problematic. So chapter 3 will examine biblical understandings of how prophecy worked, as well as the problem of false prophets and prophecy. Then chapter 4 addresses some postbiblical developments, perhaps most surprisingly that first the ancient (early postbiblical) rabbis redefined prophecy and Scripture (Torah) in a revolutionary way. Sacred texts rather than prophets became authoritative. The rabbis actually declared the age of prophecy over. Christianity, early on, and then Islam, arguably for similar reasons, each also declared the age of prophecy past once their new prophet was no longer on the scene—though no one has ever been able to stop later religious groups from claiming that now they too had a new prophet. That is the problem with prophecy: it is inherently destabilizing and unverifiable ("Why should I listen to what you say?! — God told me!"). It is interesting to speculate, in light of modern cognitive studies, how people— brilliant people, like most of the scriptural prophets, or ordinary folks in our own day—might genuinely believe God talked to them? We will consider some speculations. The literary achievement, and the moral and theological depth, of what the classic prophets produced is no less brilliant if we think of it as the product of their own reaching for God, though not (if God is a philosophical idea and not a thinking being) a message from an ultimate creator and judge.

There is more to Scripture than prophecy, and there are revelations which are not literary or even verbal. Chapter 5 turns to revelation more broadly. If *revelation* is what *reveals* God to us in the sense of making us aware of, making us think we have encountered, God, holiness, the transcendent encompassing—or the essence within—all (we stutter; it is ineffable, beyond language to capture), what else have people found revelatory? We are also accustomed to looking to God for a sense of *purpose* in our lives, a gut feeling that despite its transiency life has significance, positive *meaning*. The chapter considers what sorts of experience evoke such convictions in us?

My thinking about the impact of the way our brains work on religious belief and practice has continued to evolve since I wrote my first book. Chapter 6 subtly updates my views on faith, and considerably expands my understanding of the importance and workings of religious ritual. In *Our Religious Brains* I suggested that life is so full of potential pitfalls that our brains developed a coping mechanism—faith. You cannot know, for instance, that the bridge you are crossing is not suddenly going to collapse because of metal fatigue or a seismic tremor. We take the usual constancy of the world for granted, a mental heuristic—a matter of faith. Faith is reasonable when it does not contradict the evidence even though it goes a bit beyond the evidence. I have come to realize separating such routine faith from religious faith is the classic "distinction without a difference." Some may not want to apply the metaphor "God" to the order of being, but all are equally blessed that we evolved out of that order, acting on its usual constancy, but occasionally surprised by what to our minds seem inconsistencies. There are good surprises too, we should note. When the bridge shifts but does not quite collapse before we get off, or someone grabs us just as we begin to plummet, we exclaim, "It's a miracle!" If we are committed to the scientific worldview, however, we know our good fortune no less than our bad fortune is part of the natural order, not a divine suspension of the laws of nature.

Chapter 6 contains a further cognitive studies insight. Pondering neuroscientist Antonio Damasio's research demonstrating that "all emotions use the body as their theater,"[1] I was struck one day by the wisdom of countless rituals. Religious rituals routinely have the faithful bowing, walking,

---

1. Damasio, *Feeling of What Happens*, 51.

dancing, lifting arms heavenward, smelling spices or incense, etc., bodily acting out and not only intellectualizing about our beliefs. As spirituality contains a great deal of emotion, physical rituals have great power to move us spiritually.

As religion, then, is powerful for its emotional as well as intellectual impact, we need to ask what a philosophical God concept means for our sense of being commanded to behave in certain ways. Chapter 7 looks both at moral commandments—"You shall not murder" (Exod 20:13) and "You shall love your neighbor as yourself" (Lev 19:18), for example—and at ritual commandments, such as "Remember the Sabbath day to keep it holy" (Exod 20:8) or "seven days you shall eat unleavened bread" (Exod 12:15). In what sense, if any, does the order of being *command* anything? For religion to be a guide for life and society, not just a bland "heritage" but something to be passionately devoted to, requires an ongoing discipline. Once God's verbal commanding through prophets is recognized as myth (stories expressing our values), are commandments mandatory any longer? Moral commandments, but not ritual ones, we might go so far as to call corollaries of God's nature. Furthermore, twentieth-century Jewish theologian Mordecai Kaplan, with a philosophical God concept, argued that commandments in general developed over the ages as expressions of the community's values. For Kaplan the authority of the commandments—ritual ones, too—comes from the people and its history, not from God. They are mandatory for those who consider themselves part of the people.

We greatly extend the importance of passionate commitment in chapter 8, which takes on the dream of ultimate redemption in the indefinite "messianic" future. It is helpful to see how revolutionary it was to conceive of history as having a goal, rather than just being an account of the endlessly repeating cycles of nature, including the human life cycle. With one God rather than multiple squabbling gods, history may be conceived as linear, moving from creation to the end-time. This is clearly mythic rather than literal (what existed before the beginning and what will happen after the end?!). But it is genuinely important, a breakthrough in cultural history, to reach some consensus, at least within each religion, about what the end should be, for once there is a goal there can be progress. In the Abrahamic family of religions (Judaism, Christianity, Islam) the key goal is peace, harmony, and justice. Other goals, including overcoming death, may be added. Even those who believe the Messiah has already come recognize that peace and harmony have yet to be realized. The problem is at least in part human nature, our innate selfishness and aggression. But compassion and love are also hardwired within us. Peace and harmony? I suggest that if we agree on the goal it is not essential to achieve it fully. We have our direction, and our struggling towards it lends meaning to our lives. In this case the God concept defines the goal: Despite potential chaos and destruction—among the threats, thermonuclear weapons and global warming—we can work towards order, in part by manifesting such divine intangibles as justice, courage, truth, and peace. Secularism will not bolster our faith in that mission. Religion can if we will embrace it.

My conviction that the many doubters and self-proclaimed atheists I have found in congregations over the years are mostly *not* atheists motivated me to write this book. The problem of faith in this secular age is a confusion of metaphors. Not only those committed to the God they understand in personal terms, but we who conceive of God more abstractly, and even the doubters, stand in awe of the natural universe and share belief in love, beauty, compassion, and indeed a kaleidoscope of "divine intangibles" that developed with our universe and our human consciousness. Living in harmony with the order should be a sacred quest for each of us and all of us.

1

The Personal God Is in Trouble

God has problems. Or at least our idea of the classic, biblical, theistic God, Creator-Commander-Parent-Judge, has problems. The notion that God is a superperson who talks and listens to "his" children, who not only created and judges, and rewards and punishes, and is omniscient, omnipotent and omnibenevolent (all-knowing, all-powerful, and all-good) is in big trouble in America and other Western societies. This chapter will examine why that is the case theologically and culturally, setting the stage for a more abstract, philosophical idea of God. At first blush some traditionalist readers might find that shocking. In fact, though, at least in the Jewish world, and to a large degree in Christianity and Islam as well (the three are a "family" of historically related religions), even traditionalists readily recognize that God is not literally a person, for people have bodies and die; God does not. God as a person is a metaphor which expresses many people's experience of God. (Christians, of course, do speak of a human "incarnation" of God, but that was for a brief period two thousand years ago, and some theologians do not understand that literally, but rather take it as a myth pointing beyond itself to deeper truths about God.[1]) Our understanding of God as a superperson is not the only option, though admittedly it is the most popular. There are other metaphors which express other aspects of our subjective experience.

1. Tillich, *Dynamics of Faith*, 41–54.

Moses asserts that "the Lord your God is a consuming fire" (Deut 4:24), and likens God's choosing the people Israel to "an eagle who rouses his nestlings, / Gliding down to his young, / So did He spread out His wings and take him, / Bear him along on His pinions" (Deut 32:11). David sings, "O God, the rock wherein I take shelter: My shield, horn of my rescue, my fortress and refuge!" (2 Sam 22:3) Jeremiah twice condemns the people for forsaking God, "the Fount of living waters" (Jer 2:13 and 17:13).

No metaphor is perfect. But anthropomorphic God talk (presenting God in human terms) has become increasingly problematic. In this first chapter we shall consider three serious challenges to personal God theism. First, in the next section we see that the notion of God as person-like was problematic even in antiquity and remains so today. A benevolent deity should presumably not allow injustice and evil, which are depressingly real in our experience. Second, we shall explore more modern problems undermining the idea of God as not only creator, but active manager promulgating laws, then supervising, guiding, rewarding and punishing. Science has explained a great deal (though still not all) of how the world works, rendering God-as-creator-and-active-manager, sometimes called "the God of the gaps," less and less necessary as the gaps in our knowledge shrink. Third, all this has partnered with the rise of secularism, a political and sociological as well as intellectual force, in shoving God aside, as it were, from a central role in many people's worldview.

EVIL: WOULD A JUST AND LOVING GOD ALLOW THE INNOCENT TO SUFFER?

No statement, theological or otherwise, should be made that would not be credible in the presence of the burning children.[2]

—IRVING GREENBERG

The foundation of Jewish monotheism—and thus of Christian monotheism, as well, since Jesus and the early leaders of what became Christianity were Jews—is the Hebrew Bible. Most biblical authors clearly believed that God, after creating the world, gave commandments so that we would know what God required of us. Deuteronomy makes clear time and again that if the people faithfully obey the commandments,

2. Greenberg, "Cloud of Smoke," 23.

[God] will favor you and bless you and multiply you; He will
bless the issue of your womb and the produce of your soil, your
new grain and wine and oil, the calving of your herd and the
lambing of your flock, in the land that He swore to your fathers
to assign to you. . . . The Lord will ward off from you all sickness;
. . . You shall destroy all the peoples that the Lord your God
delivers to you. (Deut 7:13, 15, 16)

If they do not obey the commandments, on the other hand, the opposite will
transpire (Deut 8:19; or see Deut 28 for an even more vivid list of the rewards of righteousness and the devastating consequences of disobedience).
As early as the cycle of Abraham stories in Genesis we see such punishment
taking place, as when Sodom and Gomorrah are destroyed for their sinful-
ness (Gen 18:16–19:29). Later in the Torah Egypt defies God and suffers
plagues (Exod 7–12), and the Hebrews suffer plagues and other punishments for rebellion as they wander in the wilderness (see Exod 32:35, Num
11:33, Num 15:36–45 and Num 25, *inter alia*).

Even in biblical times, however, there were already those who questioned this as simplistic. What of infants and toddlers struck by lethal diseases, and whole communities falling victim to war and natural disasters?
And were there not, then as now, upstanding adults who suffered and died,
and—no less an injustice—sinners of many varieties allowed to enjoy the
fruits of their sin? The God who was believed to reward righteousness
and punish sin needed defending by the faithful. Thus was born a genre
of argument which continues today, the theodicy, a defense of God against
the charge of injustice, which in theory God should not allow, much less
perpetrate. We have two major theodicies in the book of Job. In the brilliant
poetry which comprises forty of its forty-two chapters, we meet Job, who
insists time and again that he has led a righteous life, demanding to know
why God is afflicting him. His companions insist that even to argue is a
sin, and that Job must have committed other crimes even if he does not
remember or acknowledge them, for God, virtually by definition, could not
be unjust. But Job, convincingly to most readers, refuses to acknowledge any
sin serious enough to justify his physical and psychological suffering. To the
contrary, he has been an upstanding citizen, loving his family, treating his
servants well, and showing compassion to the afflicted. He demands that the
Judge of all give him a hearing, and finally God responds from a whirlwind:

Where were you when I laid the earth's foundations
Speak if you have understanding.
Do you know who fixed its dimensions
Or who measured it with a line?

> Onto what were its bases sunk?
> Who set its cornerstone
> When the morning stars sang together
> And all the divine beings shouted for joy? (Job 38:4–7)

God goes on: Has Job been to the depths of the sea? Does he understand how the weather works? Is it by his wisdom that lions, oxen, and horses have such strength? Do hawks and eagles "soar at [his] command"? God's response goes on in this manner this until Job admits his ignorance:

> See, I am of small worth; what can I answer You?
> I clap my hand to my mouth.
> I have spoken once, and will not reply;
> Twice, and will do so no more. (Job 40:4–5)

But God, angry to have been confronted by this ignorant mortal, goes on for two more chapters! Job finally concludes the encounter, not only admitting ignorance but also dropping his case against God: "Indeed, I spoke without understanding / Of things beyond me, which I did not know. . . . Therefore, I recant and relent, / Being but dust and ashes" (Job 42:3, 6)

Read as the poem that Job mostly is, the answer to our questioning of God's justice is precisely that we are too ignorant to understand divine justice. That is not really an answer at all. "Shut up!" says God, "You cannot hope to understand, but I know what I'm doing!" A later and less poetically gifted author apparently found that too blunt, or perhaps inadequate for its failure to answer the question of why Job, and the rest of us, sometimes seem to suffer unjustly. So he added a prose frame around the poem that does give an answer. It has also been pointed out that the poem does not refer back to the details of the prologue, which has its own charm and its own answer, but diminishes the force of the poet's argument. In the first two chapters Job is, indeed, a model of righteousness of whom God is proud. But "the Adversary," essentially the heavenly prosecuting attorney, says that Job is only so good because God has blessed him so abundantly. This Adversary gets divine permission to test Job, to take away his money and his family, later even his health, claiming that Job then "will blaspheme You to Your face" (Job 1:9–12 and 2:5–6). By this logic, whether Job passes the test or not, God's apparent injustice is accounted for, and the whole story becomes "the product of divine caprice."[3] Job's protestations anger God, provoking the Voice from the Whirlwind's denunciation, but Job never curses, or loses faith in, God (Job 38–41). So in the prose epilogue Job is given twice the wealth, ten children, and lives to 140! (Job 42:10–17) Implicitly, when

---

3. Sandmel, *Hebrew Scriptures*, 276–78 and 299–300.

others of us are tested by disaster and suffering, we should know that God tests the righteous, but that like Job we will be rewarded if we hold on to our faith. This is, indeed, an answer, and rabbinic tradition strengthens it a bit by suggesting that just as a potter taps his finished works to be sure they will not break, but would not bother to do so to vessels that are obviously cracked, God strikes only those whom God knows can stand the test. "God does not try the wicked; and whom does He try? The righteous."[4] Thus when we suffer we should know that God regards us as strong enough to manage with our suffering, and will reward us for holding on to our faith. The poem says we cannot understand, but with the prose additions we get a theodicy we can understand: God never tries us beyond our ability to rise to the challenge, and will ultimately reward us for our suffering.

Can we imagine saying that to the parents of a toddler who succumbs to cancer? For the parents this could, in theory, be a test. But that does not justify the child's suffering! When, moreover, a tsunami washes away an entire coastal town, must we not echo Abraham's challenge to God prior to the destruction of Sodom and Gomorrah, "Will You sweep away the innocent along with the guilty?" (Gen 18:23)? With both theodicies in Job (and the incidental third one against which the book rebels: perhaps the sufferer truly is a sinner and needs to examine himself further to discover the sin), we can imagine cases when each might apply. But there are plenty of times when God seems obviously guilty as charged—an innocent person has suffered or a guilty one prospered. The search for answers, therefore, continued.

Any student of theology will be able to suggest further theodicies. Perhaps God, though unable or unwilling to change the natural order for us, suffers with us. Perhaps what seems evil when it happens will eventually turn out to have been a blessing in disguise. Most every child at some point complains that a teacher, coach, or other authority figure punished everyone in a group, though he or she was innocent. "It is not fair!" the child insists. The parent tries to help the child understand the predicament of the teacher. "But it is not fair!" repeats the child. Most parents, running out of other answers, finally reply, "Life is not always fair!" True enough. But when it means that Junior, at least in his own eyes blameless, is punished, the answer may not satisfy.

If any of those theodicies satisfied our human hunger for ultimate justice, we would not keep coming up with more. But we do. For instance, without the ability to do wrong as well as right, we would be mere puppets. Free will opens up the possibility of human sin, but also the possibility of human goodness and nobility. Only with the ability to do wrong as well as

4. *Midr. Rab., Song Rab.* II.16.2; and *Gen. Rab.* XXXII.3.

right can we be morally responsible agents. We, therefore, must double and redouble our efforts not only to be good ourselves, but to join with others of good will to dry the tears of the suffering and unlock the shackles of the oppressed. Like other theodicies, that too has cases that it seems appropriate to apply it to. Yet does God not share the blame for creating us flawed? The whole topic of alleged divine injustice cannot be discussed in our era without reference to the Holocaust and other modern instances of mass, genocidal murder (Armenia, Biafra, Cambodia, and more). The issue is no different when millions perish than when one perishes. Where was God?! That we should not blame God for human sin makes some sense, at least. But what of "acts of God," as the insurance companies call them, which strike us as evil but which have no human cause? Earthquakes, hurricanes, volcanic eruptions, and so on, which destroy masses of people, the innocent with the sinful, not to mention cancers and other grave illnesses which afflict fine people—even infants and toddlers, who could not have done anything bad enough to be worthy of such punishment: life furnishes us with far too many inexplicable instances of injustice.

Ingeniously, early Jews and Christians some two thousand years ago came up with a non-falsifiable theodicy. There really is justice eventually. After we die, they came to believe, we resume our existence in another realm where God, as ultimate Judge, will give us our just deserts, punishing the worst sinners and rewarding the righteous. In extreme form this becomes heaven and hell, but we need not be detained by the endless speculations about the exact nature of the world beyond (Would God really torture people eternally? Would it not be boring lounging in paradise forever?), for there is not a shred of evidence about any of it. No one can ever prove a given theory of the hereafter false. But it all sounds suspiciously like wishful thinking, denying the reality of death. No one knows. No one can know. For no one returns again to this world to tell us. Dostoevsky's Ivan Karamazov, though, tells horrible tales of suffering children, for the issue is clearest with children, he says, though "of the other tears of humanity with which the earth is soaked from its crust to its centre" the case could also be made. One story is that of a five-year-old little girl subject to unspeakable cruelty by her own parents, who beat her "until her body was one big bruise," then left her in the outhouse in the cold, smeared with feces, overnight. Another is of a cruel general from the era of serfdom in Russia who finds that an eight-year-old serf boy has thrown a stone which wounded the paw of the general's favorite hound. The next morning, while all the servants watch, his mother is brought to the front of the crowd, the boy stripped and made to run, and the dogs set upon him to rip him to pieces. Will such events facilitate progress towards a peaceful era on earth in the indefinite future? Or would there be meaningful atonement if the little girl's parents in the first instance, or the general in the second, were punished in hell after death? "What good can hell do, since those children have already suffered? And what becomes of harmony, if there is hell?" Nothing we can imagine for the future, Ivan insists, and his religious brother must admit, could justify such suffering.[5]

Need I add that a million of the six million Jewish Holocaust victims were children, and other genocides add millions more? The logic of the theodicy puzzle does not change when the scope of the evil grows, but no longer can it be dismissed, in any given case, as a rare aberration. The epigraph at the beginning of this section refers to children torn from their mothers' arms at Auschwitz, the mothers gassed and the children thrown alive into the crematoria, their agony saving the Nazis less than a penny each.[6] Neither heaven nor hell, even if real, which we cannot know, lets either humans, or a God who consciously created people capable of such vicious behavior, off the hook. Some hold on to faith anyway. Others, to put it mildly, are troubled.

My approach to faith, which is so tied up with our sense of meaning and purpose in our lives, is that it may take us beyond the evidence we find, for we certainly do not and probably never will understand all of existence. At the same time, in our day faith must not contradict scientific evidence. Individuals, obviously, may believe what they wish, but if the belief contradicts what we know of life and the world, we should not expect others to agree to it—least of all our children, whom we send off to fine schools to learn critical thinking and the scientific method. Thus, for example, you may say that the moon is made of green cheese, but that will only betray your ignorance. "How do you know?" someone is bound to ask, and you will need demonstrable facts or at least a line of reasoning that makes your belief a possible explanation of the nature of the moon given the information that we have. This is another way in which the scientific worldview has in some very important ways led us to rethink some classic religious ideas. One cannot in our time reasonably say that God created the world in six days, which does not mean that God could not have been involved in creation. Even scientists do not all agree on "why there is something rather than nothing." Elsewhere I have argued that the soul is part of consciousness, a metaphor for our sensitivity rather than a metaphysical add-on to our bodies.[7] It is entirely appropriate to argue either side of the case, however, because the

5. Dostoevsky, *Brothers Karamazov*, 250–55.

6. Greenberg, "Cloud of Smoke," 9–10.

7. Mecklenburger, *Our Religious Brains*, 61–75.

existence of souls has not been proven or disproven. Faith taking us beyond the evidence: yes. Faith contradicting the evidence: no.

THE ADVANCE OF SCIENCE AND THE SHRINKING GOD

The observable universe isn't just an arbitrary collection of stuff obeying the laws of physics—its stuff that starts out in a very particular kind of arrangement, and obeys the laws of physics thereafter. By "starts out" we are referring to conditions near the Big Bang, a moment about 14 billion years ago.[8]

—Sean Carroll

Imagine what a contemporary dermatologist might have done for poor Job, sitting on his dung heap covered in boils. But of course antibiotics were not developed until the twentieth century. So many things that enhance our lives were not invented until centuries after biblical times: mass-produced books (fifteenth century), inoculations against disease (sixteenth century in China and eighteenth in Europe), internal combustion engines (nineteenth century), commercially practical electric light bulbs (nineteenth century), airplanes, orbiting satellites, computers and the Internet (twentieth century) and lots more. There is more to learn about ourselves and the universe, of course, but we know more than the author of Job ever dreamed of knowing. Think of the questions posed by the divine Voice from the Whirlwind. We know about geological strata, tectonic plates and other aspects of "the foundations of the world." We know how weather works, how babies develop in the womb, how lions, oxen, horses, hawks and eagles evolved, and we even know that some of the beasts over which the Job poet rhapsodizes—behemoth and leviathan—are mythical. We are unlocking secrets the Job poet never thought to include, among them the structure of matter, and how to repair or even replace organs, joints and other systems in our own bodies. The list goes on and on.

The flowering of knowledge, and its increasing availability to all via media, from books and libraries to computers and the Internet, had the unintended consequence of challenging God and Scripture as the prime sources of knowledge. How did the world come into existence, and how did we—with our sometime nobility and sometime depravity—come on

8. Carroll, *Big Picture*, 43.

the scene? Various religions have offered different origin stories, but they agreed on the basic answer: God or gods did it! In Genesis, of course, God separated land and sea (Gen 1:9), created the sun to rule by day and the moon by night (Gen 1:16), provided for reproduction of each species (Gen 1:12, 22), cast rainbows across the skies (Gen 9:13) and so on and so forth. As we have seen in Job and could see in many biblical passages, people understood little as religions were getting started. But that was alright, for what people could not account for God was believed to be taking care of. Theologians have dubbed this God idea "the God of the gaps." In the last several centuries the God of the gaps has become the incredible shrinking God as human knowledge grew and grew. There remains, of course, plenty we do not know. What is "dark matter," to name but one telling example, which astrophysicists tell us is more than 80 percent of the universe?! But what we know we do not know is now commonly regarded as what science is likely to explain in due time, not a mystery inexplicable without the Divine, pulling the rug out from under those of naive faith.

If we want to say—and I do!—that every level of creation is wondrous and fascinating, from subatomic particles to worlds, galaxies and the universe, then we can still say that the whole shebang is awe inspiring, even spiritually uplifting. What we can no longer say is that God must consciously operate each part of it moment by moment. That is, for instance, tornados do not occur when God decides to send one, but when certain meteorological conditions coincide. We have gone from knowing next to nothing of how nature functions to knowing a great deal, leaving the God of the gaps with less and less to do, or—to say the same thing—leaving us with less and less need of God to explain things.

PLURALISM AND SECULARISM

The forces of secularization have no serious interest in persecuting religion. Secularization simply bypasses and undercuts religion and goes on to other things. It has relativized religious worldviews and thus rendered them innocuous. Religion has become privatized.[9]

—Harvey Cox

The problem of evil, as we have seen, is hardly new. Apparently, though, there has been sufficient goodness that most Jews, Christians and Muslims could believe that a loving God was with us, and justice would prevail, if

9. Cox, *Secular City*, 2.

not always in this world, then in an imagined next world. Likewise, human efforts to understand how the world works are not new. Technological breakthroughs enhanced people's lives. Only in recent centuries, though, has our scientific knowledge snowballed so rapidly that we begin to think the world and universe are like a self-propelled mechanism, not in need of a superintelligence to account for them. What appear to have changed, then, are the scale of evil and the pace of change.

We need to add another current to the problem of evil and the rise of science. As individuals grew up and were taught by parents, clergy and other teachers that the life they were living was the way God intended things to be, they mostly took current governmental, economic and social systems for granted. Some were richer and more powerful, others less so. Few read philosophy or other abstract ideas (if they could read at all!), but each culture passed along its mythic stories expressing their values and their notions of how life and the world worked, or at least how they should, with God invoked in various Scriptures for evidence and authority. There is plenty of profound wisdom in such books and their commentaries still. Yet with the virtual explosion of knowledge, communication and education, flaws in the social fabric seem to have become more obvious. The received wisdom, political as well as theological, came into question. Again, it is not as if no one ever had qualms in the past, but the scale, and perhaps the urgency, of modern challenges to traditional ways seems to have grown. As we shall see, in the Enlightenment religious tradition as well as society's structure came to be perceived as open to human critique and improvement—or ignoring. Secularism had been born.

Secularism, at least implicitly and often explicitly, denies that God and Scripture are or should be the major sources of truth in one's life. Reason and thus science, to which all have equal access and claim, are more important. Secularism need not be atheistic, though it can be. Historically it has both philosophical and political roots in Europe. Eighteenth-century Enlightenment thinkers such as Locke, Voltaire and Rousseau saw the church and aristocracy as monopolizing power in their mutual support. Enlightenment thinkers wanted equal rights for all. Everyone should be free not only to think what they wish, but to express their ideas and practice their religion without fear of persecution. This sounds mild today, but struck the aristocracy and the official religious leaders as radical and threatening. When put into practice politically—and this was a long struggle with steps forward and back, not just a sudden leap forward—religious freedom and human rights liberated religious minorities. The goal was freedom to believe or not believe as the individual thought best, not to undermine faith. But—and this is our major point here—this made religious doubt, and non-participation in prayer and other ritual, licit.

In ages past royalty claimed "divine right" to govern, often with religious authorities' blessing. Different religions and denominations, each claiming knowledge superior to the others, held sway in different lands, where they were apt to discriminate against and even persecute those who did not share their beliefs. Some who believed they had the one true faith, moreover, felt righteous conquering other kingdoms to save people from alleged ignorance and damnation. In the wake of the Protestant Reformation of the sixteenth century there were religious wars, most notably the Thirty Years War in the seventeenth century (1618–1648), which produced massive casualties. Enlightenment thinkers in Europe, of course, realized this must stop, and their American heirs, trying to unite into one nation immigrants from multiple realms and thus of multiple religions, had an even greater need for what came to be known as church-state separation. "Founding fathers" Jefferson, Franklin, Adams, Madison and others spoke seriously of God as Creator, and of divine "providence" (God's benevolent will for nature and human destiny). Religion, moreover, they saw as often a good influence on people, shaping character and thus good citizenship. They had no intention of undermining religion, only of keeping religion separate from government to minimize conflict and respect individual conscience.[10]

Today's secularism has been shaped by less philosophical influences, as well. As opportunities arose for Jews to more fully participate and prosper in the more open societies of nineteenth-century Europe, in Germany "[t]he wealthy found in their material goods a security that substituted for the faith of earlier generations." In nineteenth-century England ritual observance among Jews had already been on the decline since prosperity began to advance the century before, and in the same period for most French Jews synagogue attendance became the exception, not the norm.[11] Such secularization continues.

Furthermore, science and technology—commuter trains and superhighways, high-rise buildings and elevators, ample energy for lighting, food refrigeration, elevators, and so on—have made possible larger and larger cities, mass society made up of individuals and groups of diverse racial, ethnic and religious backgrounds living in close proximity.[12] Whereas once, in many cultures, a religion was the glue that kept everything together, and religious faith the basis of that, now mass society throws together people

10. Meacham, *American Gospel*, 8 and 21.

11. Meyer, *Response to Modernity*, 172.

12. Cox, *Secular City*, 5.

of widely differing backgrounds. Mutual respect and toleration, pluralism rather than parochialism, become the ideal.

Today, I suggest, clergy of many denominations would likely join me in the observation that increasingly the occupations and leisure activities of society at large—we even call it "secular society"—have become more and more effective competition to the activities of churches and synagogues. It has become increasingly difficult, for instance, to get children, especially those involved in soccer, football and other sports, to weekend religious school. Their parents and other adults, similarly, may find movies, concerts and golf games, or the ubiquitous television offerings, more attractive than the worship services they might have frequented more regularly in earlier years.

The impact of secularization becomes more vivid when we review a few of the findings of the Pew Research Center's Religion and Public Life surveys of 2007 and 2014. In 2007 83 percent of Americans identified with a generally recognized religious group (e.g., Christian, Jewish, Hindu, etc.). By 2014 that number was down dramatically to 64.5 percent, and when cross-referenced by age it is clear that the decline is mostly attributable to younger cohorts being less religious. Those who do not identify with any religious group, the so-called "Nones," have grown from 22 percent of the population to 33 percent. When looking at those who do identify with a religious group, as a rabbi I have to note that Jews are among the most secularized. The more recent study shows that across all groups 68 percent say religion is very important to them and 62 percent say they attend worship services (e.g., church or synagogue) regularly. Among mainline Protestants those numbers decline to 53 percent and 52 percent, and for Jews the numbers are 35 percent and 34 percent. Where faith is concerned, 83 percent of Americans say they believe in God "absolutely" or are "fairly certain," including 91 percent of mainline Protestants, but only 64 percent of Jews.[13] Among Jews, solidly middle class as a community and overwhelmingly college educated, about two thirds profess some faith, but only one third care enough about that faith to attend worship regularly.

Unlike Christianity, which is specifically a faith-based community, Jewish identity is peoplehood based as well. Those born Jewish remain so whether or not they join a synagogue, attend worship services or even believe in God. Thus the statistics on Jews do not necessarily mean that, as a group, Jews are about to disappear. They do, however, suggest that where secularization is concerned we are "leading the parade." If the old saw is valid that "Jews are like everyone else, only more so," the continuation of

---

13. Pew Forum, "Religious Landscape Study."

these trends will continue to threaten, increasingly, our Christian and Muslim neighbors, as well. *A perfect storm of post-Holocaust disillusionment with the sort of personal God theism much classic Scripture, and most prayer books, take for granted, the advance of science and technology (clipping the wings, as it were, of the God of the gaps) and the growth of secularism have imperiled and undermined faith in the personal God.*

What becomes of God and religion in secular societies? People hold on to their beliefs and practices to the extent they find them sustaining, but many feel less bound to them. On a day-to-day basis, even a month-to-month or year-to-year basis, many ignore religion. Times of loneliness and loss, or joy and exaltation, may be more difficult to get through without benefit of religious values and community; but houses of worship and their clergy are still available, generally, for "marryin' and buryin.'" Those who do not find that they want religious practice can opt out entirely, or make financial contributions but absent themselves from religious activities except when they personally have a need (religious affiliation, in this latter case, has been called "spiritual insurance"). With less need of a God to explain the world, and less confidence that God gives everyone their just deserts, there seems little to be lost staying home from worship, Bible study, or other religious endeavors. Religion, of course, is also about other things—morality, meaning and purpose for people's lives, a sense of connection to the Divine, the warmth of community, and so forth. Nonetheless, secularism erodes religious participation.

In sum, secularism's history helps us understand why, for better or worse in different cases, it arose. A multicultural society and intellectual freedom need the openness which secularism can engender. Those who blend into the amorphous mass are not so much hostile to religion as simply apathetic. Others remain nominally identified with a religion but give it little thought and less time. Many continue to support financially the religious institutions they attend but rarely. They desire, we may infer, to pass along their religious identity and traditions to their children, and turn to churches, synagogues and clergy for guidance and blessing at life's high and low points—births, children's maturation (bar/bat mitzvah, quinceañera, confirmation), weddings and deaths. That sociological observation, though, begs for theological analysis. If people care about their religious heritage, which many, though obviously not all, do, and their various faiths call for regular public worship, why is prayer participation so low? As we will see in chapter 6, I think a misunderstanding of the role of public prayer is part of the problem. But there is no evading the deeper issue. In light of all the challenges to faith, if religion is to serve our human hunger for meaning, we need to rethink our understanding of God.

2

God

An It, Not a He

The world is charged with the grandeur of God.
It will flame out, like shining from shook foil; . . .[1]

—GERARD MANLEY HOPKINS

I begin with an uncommon assertion: God is not a conscious being. God does not have a mind. Growing up in the Western world, whether or not you come from a religious household, you can scarcely help coming to think of God as personal, by which I mean person-like. In the classic theist telling ("theism" being the theory that God is person-like, or perhaps we should say superperson-like, the ultimate king/father/creator/commander/redeemer/ judge), God is the perfect source and exemplar of every virtue, worthy of reverence, imitation and even fear (this is surely not someone you want to get on the bad side of!). This theistic God, exhibiting power and wisdom, though on a grander scale than any mere person—"the King, the King of kings, the Holy One, praised be He," as Jewish liturgy puts it—is enough like us—thinking, judging, creating, caring—that we can identify with him and imagine ourselves in the divine image (Gen 1:26), the highest of compliments. Along with not being limited by a frail and perishable body (except,

1. Hopkins, "God's Grandeur."

14

in the Christian mind, for Jesus two thousand years ago), God is perfect in knowledge, wisdom and power.

So the first thing we need to talk about is the birth of that ubiquitous God idea. It is important to say "God idea" and not simply "God" because there are other God ideas. Among many possible examples, God has been conceived of as order or "ground" of being (my preferred image), first cause, process-in-history, process working for good, and mathematical perfection of the universe. Pantheists (including most mystics) think God and the universe are one and the same, so that God is nature and everything is holy, and for panentheists that God includes but also goes beyond the universe.[2] Still, most classic Western religious believers think of God as personal, which, ironically, is tremendously appealing emotionally even as, for many, it is an obstacle to faith rationally. The very fact that every culture comes up with some sort of manifestation of divinity or holiness suggests that there is something in human nature which leads us there. I will argue that something in the way humans think, something in the nature of our brains, leads us to believe in powerful gods or God, though we cannot "see" divinity in the way we see one another. We crave meaning, a sense that something beyond ourselves entails order, at least, and perhaps purpose. That sense can be provided by faith in a God who or which is responsible for the way things are.

Can we hold on to personal God theism despite the problems we saw in chapter 1? Of course. We can simply ignore the problems, arguing, with early-third-century church father Tertullian, *credo quia absurdum est*, "I believe because it is absurd." Tertullian's point was that what Scripture says which strains credibility should be taken on faith; one does not *need* faith for what can be known rationally. But this is not even mainstream Catholic doctrine any more, and is certainly profoundly un-Jewish, with our Talmudic tradition of struggling to show that religion makes sense. Perhaps more promising for explaining seeming contradictions in theism is what has been called Maimonides' *via negativa*. Maimonides, a twelfth-century Aristotelian, taught that God is so utterly unique that we cannot make an analogy between God and anything we know in our own experience. All we can say of God is what God is *not* (e.g., even to say God exists implies incorrectly

---

2. Panentheism would be an appealing idea, with God fully immanent in our experience because everything is God, yet also transcendent, if it did not run contrary to modern science. Counterintuitive though it may be, modern science holds that the universe began with a "Big Bang" out of a tiny speck, and from that primal speck the universe expanded, and most would say continues to expand, to its huge size today. The universe is not expanding into space outside itself, but encompasses all that is. To speak of anything outside the universe is thus incoherent. See Nelson, *Judaism, Physics and God*, 7–8.

that God exists as we exist, so we may only say God does not *not* exist). That at first has appeal, for it implies that we can say God does not have thoughts as we do, leaving open the possibility of God having some uniquely divine sort of thoughts. But what would they be? We may perceive of God as loving and just, but only because "loving and just" in the divine context mean something different than we mean by them. How would we, in an age of science, test if such love and justice (or even existence) are not figments of our imaginations? We can scarcely expect that to satisfy a scientifically educated modern person that religious and scientific understandings of reality are compatible. So I ask readers unaccustomed to thinking of God other than as a conscious being to consider, at least for sake of argument, a philosophical, non-personal idea of God.

The genre of stories of gods in different cultures is known as mythology, as in Greek mythology, Norse mythology, Hebrew mythology, and so on. It is flattering and tempting for many to think that "my religion has the true story, while other religions and cultures teach myths." But in cross-cultural comparison myth does not mean merely imaginative, fictional tales. Myths carry in story form the basic values each culture holds dear. So, for instance, the creation myth of Genesis 1:1—2:4 moderns know to be false as science and thus invalid as history. Most likely that first biblical creation story was selected by biblical editors to lead off the first book of the Bible to bear witness that our world was initiated by God and is a good place. God declares aspects of creation good seven times in one chapter! The authors found the world's design impressive, as well, with lights for night and for day, plants ingeniously including the seeds of reproduction in each species, and humans topping off the process and—like God!—deserving a rest after each week's work. The point is not that any of this is literally true as history or science, but to make values statements that became our Judeo-Christian-Islamic view of life and the world. Though subsequent generations, with new experiences and knowledge, have repeatedly reinterpreted the original text, it serves as an anchor so our understandings do not drift totally away from the initial thrust, namely, that the world is God's and thus good.

One further preliminary thought before addressing the birth of the God idea, a point that deserves to be stated explicitly though hardly anyone would disagree: much though we have learned over the ages, no mere mortal, with our limited understanding, fully comprehends the infinite, cosmic God. In the modern, scientific epoch we are more apt to default to empirically based theories than to values-based myths for knowledge of why things are as they are. But in neither personal nor philosophical theologies do we pretend to have adequate language, much less complete enough understanding, to claim to give precise definitions and descriptions of God.

Every God idea is an approximation, expressible only in figurative or poetic language, not literal description. As we shall see, it is entirely understandable that one of the metaphors people use for God is the personal metaphor. As we saw in chapter 1, however, that metaphor is so flawed that it should not be relied upon exclusively if we want to have an idea of God acceptable to modern, university-educated, critical thinkers.

THE ORIGIN OF GOD(S)

The pantheon of a complex civilization like Sumer was not simple. There were many components to the identity of a god: natural, political, cultural, and familial. In part, gods represented the power felt in the universe. They ordered, regulated, and controlled the natural elements: the sky, sun, moon, storms, and stars. In this way, all aspects of the cosmos that were significant to the life of humans were supervised and determined. Because of the gods' supervision, the world was not chaotic. Those same gods that controlled nature also supervised the polis.[3]

—TIKVA FRYMER-KENSKY

We can imagine an early shepherd arriving with his small flock at the creek only to find scarcely a trickle of water—even less than yesterday! His sheep will die, he realizes, unless rain comes soon. "Oh clouds, bring us rain! Oh stream, run with abundant water!" he pleads. Nothing happens immediately, but that night there is a storm, so the next day he returns with the flock and finds at least some water. "Thank you, clouds!" he exclaims, "And keep flowing, great stream." When water is short again, he will address these spirits again, and he tells neighbors of his successes. When future prayers fail, he will blame himself; the gods must be angry with him. When not only people and animals, but each forest or tree, stream or hill, and storm, sun, moon and constellation comes to be regarded as having its own animating spirit, that is called animism. The world seems full of spirits! Perhaps, though, our shepherd—or his family or larger culture—eventually takes a small logical leap and thinks the rains are all controlled by one great storm god. They would certainly have realized that the crops needed more than just rain. Perhaps other natural forces should be propitiated individually, or were rolled in with the rain god, keeping rain, dew, wind and insects in line.

3. Frymer-Kensky, *In the Wake of the Goddesses,* 9.

As this process repeated itself countless times, sets of gods developed and were believed to have the fate of human beings in their power. The point is not the simplistic example, but the universal habit of mind. We tend to personalize impersonal forces. I doubt anyone would mistake me for an animist or polytheist, but the microwave in my kitchen tends not to go off when I press the "stop" button, yet usually works fine for my wife—leading me to say that "this microwave oven doesn't like me." I regularly hear people say they have brought their raincoat or umbrella "so that it won't rain," as if some mischievous rain god were deciding the weather based on their preparedness.

Treating other entities, even inanimate ones, as having intentions toward us is a feature of our brains. This is even more obviously the case where animals or people are involved. We can be safer, or find food or mates more easily, if we regard their actions as aimed at us—whether or not they are. We keep our distance from a growling dog, though what is bothering the animal may have nothing to do with us. The guy who has just come into the party sees two women nearby begin to whisper to one another and wonders what they are saying about *him*. They could be talking about any number of things, of course, but his reaction is a normal habit of mind. Each of our brains, tasked by nature with getting us safely through life, finds it useful to assume that events around us are somehow aimed at us. Daniel Dennett calls this "taking the intentional stance"[4] and neuroscientist Michael Graziano says we attribute minds, awareness, to others, to people, quite obviously,[5] but also, once we develop our high level of "social awareness," to animals and far more:

> Consider human spirituality—the tendency to see spirits every-where, to see mind not only in ourselves and in each other, not only in pets and other animals, but also in cars that we get mad at when they don't start; in house plants that we talk to as we water them; in the favorite stuffed animals of children, like Hobbes of Calvin and Hobbes; in storms that seem like the products of evil spirits; in the empty spaces at night when you get the creepy irrational feeling that someone is in your house uninvited. It is really only a small step from the universal perception of mind everywhere to the more formalized notions of ghosts, angels, devils, and deities . . . even the atheistic scientists among us, such as myself, cannot help being spiritual. It is built into our social machinery. It is what people are.[6]

4. For a basic statement see Dennett, *Kinds of Minds*, 19–55.

5. Graziano, *Consciousness and the Social Brain*, 85.

6. Graziano, *Consciousness and the Social Brain*, 211–12.

Our early human ancestors attributed consciousness, and gave names, to legions of gods and goddesses, personifications—or more aptly, deifications, but their person-like qualities were of the essence—of natural forces: sun, storms, rivers, mountains and, more abstractly, fertility and wisdom, as well as cultural phenomena that seemed to have real power over them, among them cities, nations and war. Even specific talents were imagined to have conscious intent towards them, so there were gods appealed to by sandal makers, sailors, warriors, farmers and so on. The ancient world was felt as teeming with spirits. Not all were equally powerful. They could be imagined as organized into hierarchies, mirroring the experience of those whose lively imaginations called them into being as gods and goddesses. People believed that the gods played and schemed, that they fought and copulated with one another, and from time to time with mortals too. To whatever extent possible, people wanted to curry favor with the gods. Since mortal leaders enjoyed flattery, sing the gods hymns of praise! Since everyone likes to eat, the gods and goddesses could be propitiated with sacrifices of fruits, vegetables, bread, oil and meat—only the best, of course, for figures believed to hold powers of success and failure, even life and death, over their human subjects. Religious functionaries multiplied, specialists who could be counted upon to perform the sacrifices and rituals correctly.

I am not suggesting that this was necessarily the sole impetus in the birth of gods and goddesses, or institutional religions. Religion helps create a sense of identity, motivating group cooperation and cohesion. We can rally behind gods against enemies. Desire for divine reward and fear of punishment may motivate individual and group morality, reinforcing family, tribal and national solidarity, or even a sense of common humanity. Leaders can exploit religion to maintain power, collect taxes or raise an army—whether for the common good or their own greed. Religion is a chief foundation of culture, inspiring and supporting the arts. The list could go on. The point is that overarching purpose for groups is built first on the self-transcendent leap of individuals. What may well have begun in fear and self-interest can blossom in cooperation, compassion and beauty—or degrade into exploitation, manipulation or brutality.

In any event, the way our minds work, an aspect of human nature, is one of the foundations of religion. In some ways polytheism was naive. But we truly are subject to, and often in awe of, nature, the transcendent reality that includes and subsumes us. At one level we still like to give names to hurricanes, ships and weapons. In our day, though, at least in our more reflective moods, most of us know these inanimate entities are not truly separate consciousnesses. Psychologists Daniel Wegner and Kurt Gray, however, show people admitting lots of non-living entities, from blow-up plastic women to computers and robots, into what they call "the mind club."[7]

Today, long after the evolution of monotheism, when any of these imaginary spirits are deified, most would call them "false gods." But the skills and tools needed to earn our bread, build our homes and entertain us remain real enough. Other major aspects of culture, too—even wisdom and certainly war—have undeniable impact on our well-being. Neither should anyone doubt the reality of the forces of nature, but now we understand that nature operates blindly and automatically. We are part of the natural world and should be careful, indeed, with its awesome powers. But these abstractions and forces are not directed specifically—consciously, personally—at us. Imputing will to them is, and must always have been, a fallacy.

A couple of loose ends remain to tie up before we move on. What happened to the gods and goddesses? First of all, many in the world still believe in multiple gods and make idols to represent them. One of my favorite sites in Hong Kong is the Wong Tai Sin Temple, really a temple complex shared by Taoists, Buddhists and Confucianists. Entering the large grounds from the street, one is greeted by statues of fierce gods, part animal and part human, and farther in one comes to more statues, and an altar, to which the faithful bring fish and piglets as well as flowers and vegetables as offerings. This popular expression of Eastern religions is far from the philosophic Taoism of Lao Tzu's *Tao Te Ching*, or the wisdom of the Buddha or Confucius. Many temples of these and other faiths have legions of sculpted and painted images—"idols," many of us would call them—revered by many. Other numerically smaller polytheistic religions may be found 'round the world, as well.

Polytheism and idolatry are not gone. Yet the fact remains that Judaism, Christianity and Islam have won over many of the world's faithful—a majority. Monotheism, over many, many centuries, probably took over in most of the world because of a certain inherent instability in polytheism. What if you were faithful to your patron god and the crops did not grow anyway? Perhaps your god and some other were fighting, or even playing. ("As flies to wanton boys, are we to the gods. / They kill us for their sport," observed Shakespeare.[8]) If one nation, say a superpower like ancient Egypt or Assyria, conquered yours, did that mean their gods were stronger and you should be wise enough to adopt them, or—the prophetic response in Hebrew Scriptures—did it mean that your God was punishing you? In Isaiah 10:5, for instance, God declares Assyria "the rod of My wrath." In so

7. Wegner and Gray, *Mind Club*, 57–58 and 84–86.
8. Shakespeare, *King Lear*, act 4, scene 1.

many mythological stories of the gods they are capricious, which perhaps was necessary to account for the inconsistency of human experience. With one God there can be one moral order, and human fate, whether individual or group, can be explained as the result of God's judgement. As noted above, the forces the gods represented were real enough; the question we are dealing with is not whether there is anything behind the idea of gods or God, but whether there is, or even can be, a divine consciousness. *I suggest that God is not, as it were, the "author" of the order of being (physical being itself—creation—and a host of other non-physical manifestations of divinity, starting with morality), but rather the network of rules and laws itself, a collective noun as opposed to a proper name for a conscious being.*

MORE THAN THE LAWS OF SCIENCE: DIVINE INTANGIBLES

To the modern man, religion can no longer be a matter of entering into relationship with the supernatural. The only kind of religion that can help him live and get the most out of life will be the one which will teach him to identify as divine or holy whatever in human nature or in the world about him enhances human life.[9]

—MORDECAI KAPLAN

The planet earth is a wondrous place, well stocked with natural resources, blessed with magnificent vistas. We are told, moreover, that it is just the right distance from the sun not to be too hot or cold for life to thrive. Its vast supply of water can support aquatic life, as well as a water cycle that makes possible life on land. Earth is perfectly suited for human habitation. Amazing, we might think. While the manifold features both in their complexity individually and in systems (food chain, weather, and so on) are remarkable and should inspire us to take far better care of our environment than currently, we should not be too surprised at its wondrous design. We know how the planet evolved over billions of years. Darwinian evolution gives us a pretty good idea of how simple life developed into the incredible diversity and complexity of plant and animal life and, ultimately, each human being. Of course we find our world reasonably accommodating to our needs, for we coevolved with it. Had it been a little different, but still able to sustain

9. Kaplan, *Meaning of God*, 25.

life, we would likely be a little different. The world was not created for our comfort; we evolved to fit in.

It was only a moment ago on the scale of evolutionary time that we humans came on the scene and learned to examine ourselves and our environment microscopically and telescopically. We are learning more and more about the workings of energy and subatomic particles. We can look out to the heavens at other stars, solar systems and galaxies millions of light-years away. It is breathtaking to contemplate: we are both aware and intelligent enough to understand how we fit into the earth's ecology, and how our planet fits into the vast cosmos. On the one hand we cannot help being proud of our achievements, and on the other hand we know that though our world seems huge to us it is far smaller than the sun—which itself is scarcely a speck of light in a galaxy which in turn is but one of billions of them. In our own lifetime cosmologists have found other planets circling other stars. There could be thousands, even millions or billions, capable of sustaining life, though we have yet to find life on another one, for we are too small for the vast distances involved. To say that one set of laws governs all of this, from the tiniest subatomic level through the microscopic, then to our human level and on to the solar systems and galaxies of an ever-growing universe billions of light-years across, is a bold assertion, but one in which Western religions, because they posit only one God, and science, because it theorizes only one "Design Space" (a concept we shall return to shortly), concur. This is what I mean, first of all, by the order of being: not the matter and energy themselves, but the intangible, immaterial rules by which they operate. That is already a God worthy of our awe and reverence, and is not yet the whole story!

Not long ago a friend asked me what I was working on these days. I told him I was taking notes for a book on the implications for religion and modern faith of a philosophical rather than personal God concept. He pressed further on what exactly I meant, so I said I was trying to systematize my thinking on God as the structure of being, which I had mentioned without going into depth in my previous book, *Our Religious Brains*. Anyone who has studied physics or chemistry, I said, knows that there are laws which determine what will happen when various substances interact, or when they are heated or cooled. Science can also describe the inner structure of atoms, how subatomic particles interact, how different wavelengths of light are seen by us as different colors, how evolution occurs, how energy and mass can translate into one another, and so on and so forth. "Oh," he said, "you are saying that God is the laws of physics!" "Yes, for starters," I replied, "and that is important for a God concept because lots of people who think of themselves as agnostics or atheists do accept these laws, this order. Especially with quantum physics these days, there is still lots that we cannot explain. But if we simply shift the focus from God as creator of the laws by which the universe operates to God as the laws themselves, *voila!*: no one is an atheist! Furthermore, the order of being as we experience it involves more than just physical order. Before I started reading about new understandings of science I was already speaking regularly about God as a set of 'divine intangibles.' There are moral norms, ideas—yea, ideals—and all sorts of other non-physical aspects of the reality we encounter. Most of us find that these have the capacity to make life meaningful and worthwhile for us. I doubt anyone has ever developed a full list, but these are things people mostly agree are real and important, but which philosophers and other thinkers cannot fully agree on definitions of: love, beauty, justice, truth, peace and compassion. Others could be added; perhaps nobility, honesty, bravery. Even if we are not sure precisely what each is (God is never wholly understood!), we certainly recognize their absence when we suffer indifference or hatred, lies, ugliness and injustice. So start with the laws of physical reality, and add the intangible but real features of the world which move us emotionally and often excite us intellectually. Few would doubt the reality of these phenomena, however awkwardly we stammer in our attempts to define them. Roll up all these, together with the physical laws, into one collective noun for that which gives life meaning and we have 'God.'"

What I did not tell my friend in that brief, informal conversation, but which deserves mention here, is how I came to deal with two worries that I had about the adequacy of this God concept. First, is this really monotheism if so many varied aspects of reality are involved? Second, even where some of the features of physical or scientific reality are concerned, and certainly where what I have called the divine intangibles such as beauty and love are concerned, can we be sure that they are real in the world beyond our own consciousness, and not simply functions of the way our brains process information? Exploring these two questions should help clarify the concept.

FIRST WORRY: IS THIS REALLY MONOTHEISM?

The great physicist Albert Einstein spent years trying to come up with a "unified field theory" to account for physical reality with one formula "that would tie together electricity and magnetism and gravity and quantum mechanics."[10] He failed, but remained convinced that the formula would one day be found. So if we start with physical realities which may or may not be unitary, then add further intangible (we might even say "spiritual") realities,

10. Isaacson, *Einstein*, 336.

can we still call the result monotheism, not dualism or even polytheism? The answer I have satisfied myself with is twofold. It has been demonstrated that our monotheistic traditions evolved out of polytheism and even animism, lots of imagined spirits becoming one God.[11] The two most common names for God in the Hebrew Bible, *YHWH* and *Elohim*, demonstrate that history. *Elohim*, strangely, is a plural form used (but with singular verbs and adjectives) for the one God, who, in a world perceived as populated by lots and lots of gods and goddesses, needed a name, *YHWH*, to distinguish "him" from the others. Others had a pantheon of gods; Hebrews had only *YHWH*. Thus in Deuteronomy Moses declares just before the revelation at Sinai (Deut 4:35 and 4:39), and the people declare repeatedly when Elijah has bested the prophets of Baal in 1 Kings 18:39 (which Jews echo at the end of our Yom Kippur liturgy), *YHWH Hu Ha'Elohim*, contextually, "*YHWH* is God," not, of course, "*YHWH* is the gods." This is a palimpsest, the plural form of *elohim* having become singular but historically recognizable as a collective singular ("*YHWH* is the pantheon"—there is no other). Likewise the assertion which every religious Jew knows by heart from constant repetition, "Hear, O Israel, *YHWH* is our *Elohim*, *YHWH* is one" (Deut 6:4), in original historical context probably meant, "Hear, O Israel, *YHWH* is our pantheon, *YHWH* is one (not many, as our neighbors believed)." As in antiquity gods charged with various aspects of reality were conceptually unified, evolving into one God, in modernity the laws that determine the nature of different aspects of reality have been conceptually merged—though in current science not yet quite fully. These various aspects of reality, after all, interact constantly. Likewise, as we are part of nature, comprised of physical stuff ourselves, and one of our distinguishing characteristics is the ability to conceptualize, abstract and explain complexities of the universe we encounter, what our understanding adds remains part of the natural order. Reality, including *Homo sapiens*, is one system.

I might add that while some monotheists might resist the idea that God could have multiple aspects (Einstein could yet be proven correct!), rabbinic (postbiblical) Jews spoke of God having a *midut hadin* and a *midut harachamim*, distinguishable judgmental and merciful aspects,[12] and further felt that they did not often encounter the transcendent God, but rather

---

11. See Frymer-Kensky, *In the Wake of the Goddesses*, especially chapter 7, which traces how male gods assimilated the duties of the goddesses, and chapter 8, which presents such evolution uniting all divine functions into the one God, *YHWH*.

12. See Kohler, *Jewish Theology*, 126; and Moore, *Judaism*, 1:387. The most common names for God in the Torah, *YHWH* and *Elohim*, are often interpreted in rabbinic literature as referring, respectively, to God's attributes of mercy and justice.

one immanent aspect of that God, the *Sh'chinah* or "divine presence."[13] Christians, similarly, developed the idea of the Trinity—Father, Son and Holy Spirit, three aspects of one God—and did not consider themselves any less monotheistic for that. I must admit to having occasionally been amused listening to fellow Jews criticizing the Trinity as a compromise of monotheism, since, after all, the Jewish mystical tradition speaks of the godhead as divided into ten *sefirot* or "spheres" that constantly interact within God, creating and sustaining the world. In sum, I am not suggesting any greater a compromise of God's unity than previous generations' conceptions. I still recite, with no compromise of my intellect, *Shema Yisraeyl Adonai Eloheinu Adonai echad*, "Hear, O Israel, *Adonai* is our God, *Adonai* alone" (as I like to translate it for our time).

SECOND WORRY: ARE INTANGIBLES ONLY IN OUR OWN MINDS?

What about these "divine intangibles," which, whatever else or more they may be, are at least features of our subjective awareness? Consider: You and a friend agree that there are beautiful pieces of music, but she likes jazz and you like classical. Perhaps you also find one another more than a little attractive, but then so presumably do many pairs of hippopotamuses. Is this all purely subjective in each of our heads, or is there such a thing as beauty?

Some twenty years ago I had been fretting over the possibility that what I call "divine intangibles" were only features of our minds, products of the way our brains processes data about the outside world. By way of analogy, in the outside world light hits differing objects and is reflected in different wavelengths. To us some appear red, some blue, and others appear other colors. But all that is "out there" are waves of light. They have to be translated in our brains differently so that we can distinguish them, which, in Darwinian fashion, promotes survival (you might recognize a predatory animal from greater distance if it is yellow against a green or brown background, or recognize that a storm is coming when gray skies and black clouds are on the horizon rather than blue skies with perhaps a few fluffy white clouds). Then are colors real or only illusions in our own minds? We cannot, after all, be totally confident that we all mean exactly the same thing

13. Kohler, *Jewish Theology*, 197, which speaks of the gap felt between the transcendent God and the world being so great that "instead of God's own being, His reflected radiance or the power invested in His name descends from on high. . . . [The rabbis] therefore coined the word Shekinah—'the divine Condescension' or 'Presence'—to be used instead of the Deity himself."

by "green," since we cannot define it as other than a wavelength, or by simile (green like the grass, green like the forest). It seems likely that most of us mean the same thing by colors, since most find red to be "loud" or attention grabbing, and blue to be soothing or calming. But my color-blind father insisted that he and I agreed about the color of many brown things, though some of what I saw as green—the lawn, the forest—he saw as brown. Dogs are said to see the world only in shades of black and white (like black and white photography).

This complicates further when an artist paints in multiple colors and people declare the finished painting beautiful. Except while the majority agrees on its beauty, some may declare it ugly. Is beauty real? The same question applies to the night skies, or telescopic photos of galactic space, which I find gorgeous and others may yawn at. Is this "divine intangible" beauty just a feature of my mind—and yours too? There is clearly a subjective element to our judgement. Yet, though we do not necessarily agree on what is beautiful, we agree that there is such a thing as beauty. Interestingly, we should note, most of us would nod assent to the preacher who declares "love is beautiful" or the poet asserting that "beauty is truth, truth beauty." Similarly, after years of interfaith dialogue, I am used to Jews saying that justice is the most important value and Christians saying that love is. I enjoy pointing out that situational ethics thinker Joseph Fletcher declared this a meaningless quibble, for "Love and Justice are the same, for justice is love distributed, nothing else."[14] We could play this philosophical game with any of the divine intangibles, agreeing they are real enough to lend meaning to our lives without reaching total agreement on their definitions and interrelationships.

When I read philosopher of science Daniel Dennett's wonderful book *Darwin's Dangerous Idea*, I learned about Dennett's idea of "Design Space." At risk of greatly oversimplifying, but I hope this will do to get the basic idea necessary for my point here, if everything that is in our universe today started some 14.8 billion years ago with the so-called Big Bang, then everything in our universe is related by complex but inexorable descent from common ancestry. Life on Earth probably began at least 3.5 billion years ago and slowly led on to us humans. It is all one long and still-continuing process. Thus we ourselves are part of that "Tree of Life" and what we produce (trees grow leaves, termites make nests and we write books and build rockets) is also related to everything else that is. As Dennett puts it, "*there is only one Design Space, and everything actual in it is united with everything else.*"[15]

---

14. Fletcher, *Situational Ethics*, 87.

15. Dennett, *Darwin's Dangerous Idea*, time lines, 87–89; quote 135 (emphasis original).

As I pondered my theological query about the objective or merely subjective nature of "divine intangibles" and Dennett's scientific and philosophical argument, I wrote him a letter, complementing him on his fascinating book and then, more pointedly, asking:

> For years I have been teaching that while the Bible and other classic texts present God as author of peace, source of truth, commander of justice, and so on and so forth, in fact, demythologized, God is peace, truth, justice, beauty, love, creativity–the sum total of all the intangibles which make meaningful living possible. . . . What has especially worried me is the possibility that all these things which seem so real, even so sacred, to us could be real "in here" but not "out there." But when I read *Darwin's Dangerous Idea* I discovered (among other things) that "there is only one Design Space, and everything actual in it is united with everything else" (p. 135, italics yours!). If human Design Space is part and parcel of Design Space, that is a false dichotomy. (One star may not recognize the beauty of another star, but if there is such a thing as beauty which can be recognized, it is a real part of Design Space everywhere, though it takes being at a certain stage of evolution–ours!–to recognize it.)—Am I, here, forcing things which do not belong into the concept of Design Space?[16]

Dr. Dennett graciously wrote back:

> Thanks for the most thoughtful and constructive letter. You are right: "in here" and "out there" is a false dichotomy. In one way or another, that point has been at the heart of all my work for thirty years—though not expressed in just those terms. I'm particularly taken with your way of getting to the point.[17]

Dr. Dennett is still plowing this field very helpfully. In his most recent book, discussing some scholars' objection to the concept of memes, he reports that some insist that "objects in the official ontology of the scientific image really exist, but solid objects, colors, sunsets, rainbows, love, hate, dollars, home runs, lawyers, songs, words, and so on, don't really exist."[18] That is a "defensible position," he admits, and it is even a version of what he argues when he has said that colors and sunsets, and even dollars (the latter just paper and ink, or ciphers on a balance sheet, after all) are "user illusions," like the icons on your computer monitor. Those icons enable you

16. Author's files.

17. Author's files.

18. Dennett, *From Bacteria to Bach*, 222.

to see and utilize the machine sometimes as a word processor, sometimes as a movie or television projector and sometimes as a bookkeeping machine— useful illusions which help you navigate the computer's potential. They are not fictions, but useful ways of keeping track of reality. Divine intangibles, likewise, are not literal descriptions of things, but ways our brains interpret what certain experiences mean to us. As distinct from our concepts of unicorns or little green men on Mars, however, we are construing data from actual, not fictional, phenomena. This is just like our brains presenting a desk or a tree as a solid object, though from the perspective of physics they are made up of atoms each one of which contains far more space than particles. Desks and trees are not illusions, but real phenomena which our senses and our brains present to consciousness in usable ways. Beauty, truth, love, etc. are not illusions either, but vital aspects of the reality we navigate. An element of subjectivity in them is not a problem. They are not only "in here" in our brains, but have counterparts "out there" in the world.

GOD AND COGNITIVE BIAS

This notion of a philosophical God concept as opposed to a personal God concept may be clearer, or more convincing, if I contextualize it further. Our brains are always occupied with constructing and interpreting the world based partly on the input of our senses, partly on what we have learned from previous experience, and partly on a panoply of hardwired heuristics—mental techniques, shortcuts, which usually serve us well. Earlier in the chapter I suggested that the intentional stance, personalizing what goes on around us, is precisely such a technique. We would not want to escape using most of these heuristics even if we could. But since they are sometimes wrong they are also called "cognitive biases." We should remember that they are helpful, but not infallible.

Consider: When a "magician," actually an illusionist, appears to draw a coin out of someone's ear, we know that it is sleight of hand. When something suddenly appears, we assume it comes out of the place at which it appeared. So our brains "read" the scene as the coin coming out of the ear, not quickly produced from the nimble fingers. Even if you know in this case that it is an illusion, you have to tell yourself that; your visual perception still experiences it as a coin coming out of an ear because of your cognitive bias. Likewise, but more significantly for our experience of art (e.g., drawing, painting, even photography), any trained artist can produce the illusion of depth on a flat canvas or screen. At the simplest level, put smaller items behind larger ones and they appear farther away, since, in the way our visual perception works, distant objects look smaller than close objects. So even if the canvas is flat the viewer gets the impression of depth. That is enhanced if the "closer" items on the flat canvas seem to partially obscure what is to be seen (but is actually not) "behind" them. An art teacher would go on to vanishing points, but you probably get the idea. As our brains interpret sense data, they complete patterns, adjust for perspective, and so on—and not just with visual cues, but with other senses (a loud whistle, or a strong smell, seems closer than a weak one). Far from demonstrating that the brain is always getting things wrong, in fact the brain has evolved to make adjustments to get things right, effortlessly, most of the time. What these examples show is that we do not simply sense what is out there in the world; our brains start with sensory data and preprogrammed notions, then construct our perceptions.

But let's move on to cognitive biases which may impact our success, or even our survival, in life. Airplane pilots, whether of small planes or giant airliners, need to be taught that when flying in the dark, and especially in storms when ground or stars are not visible, they must not trust their instincts, their perceptions, regarding not only altitude, but even where up and down are relative to the plane they are piloting. Though they think, based on the balancing system of their ears and brains, that they are flying parallel to the ground, they must trust their instruments for this data or they are apt to feel calm and in control as they descend and crash, as is believed to have happened to the Piper plane in which inexperienced pilot John F. Kennedy Jr. crashed during a storm in July of 1999, and to Flash Airlines flight 604, a Boeing jetliner taking off from Sharm el-Sheikh at 4:44 a.m. bound for Cairo and Paris, which minutes later crashed into the Red Sea in January of 2004.[19] The balancing system of our ears and brain is one of the wonders of nature, and works for us nearly always—but "nearly" is not good enough to assume we are infallible.

One more example, demonstrating cognitive bias not only in perception, but in belief: In 2002 psychologist Daniel Kahneman won the Nobel Prize in Economics for his work on decision-making. Among the many areas he researched, Kahneman found that investment specialists think that years of experience and hours of patient analysis make them more likely than amateur investors to find stocks and other investments which will outperform the markets. We normally think that practice and hard work give us an advantage over the competition, but investment, which entails predicting the future, is not tennis or craftsmanship. Money managers and the public, Kahneman found, would normally be better off buying index

19. Sharot, *Optimism Bias*, 3–5.

funds than paying "experts" for investment advice. He reports doing presentations on this, with the data to back it up, for twenty-four wealth advisors with years of experience, and for their bosses. Their investment success was random. Each year some did better than others, of course, but over multiple years it all evened out. Both bosses and stock-pickers listened politely without seeming upset or embarrassed to be told their success or failure was luck. Why? They each assumed he was talking about the others! Their cognitive bias was so convincing to them that they each "knew" that they, with all their hard work and experience, were better than average. Furthermore, "Cognitive illusions can be more stubborn than visual illusion," for "We know that people can maintain an unshakable faith in any proposition, however absurd, when they are sustained by a community of like-minded believers."[20]

When we say "God," we are referring to the awesome and intricate order of all that exists in the universe (again: not the author of the order, but the order itself—we might say, metaphorically, the software, not the hardware, of the universe). We can start with the laws of physics, which are beyond our full understanding, but undoubtedly real and responsible for creation as we know it, both the process and the product. But there is more, including what I like to call the "divine intangibles," the reality of which make meaning and purpose possible in our lives: truth, justice, love, beauty, hope, and so on. Philosophers, psychologists, neuroscientists and others cannot fully agree amongst themselves even on the definition of each of these. On a gut level, though, we know them by experience and also, sometimes, by their lack when we suffer from falsehood, injustice, hatred, ugliness and despair. They are partly categories of our own thinking. But this need not mean they are not also inherent in the world "out there" beyond our own minds. We have been learning in recent years, for instance, about hardwired morality, and as we will discuss further in chapter 5, argument can be made for the superiority of cooperation over selfishness being built into the structure of being.

God, so conceived, is genuine. For starters, neither we nor our world would exist without it. Add further intangible aspects of existence, unquestionably real in our experience and, quite possibly in many cases, real beyond human experience as well. Put it all together and we find meaning in our lives and in the universe. All of that is part of what people have long meant when speaking of God, but none of it requires God to be a human writ large, a divine consciousness. *The theistic notion of a "personal" God results from a cognitive bias: we are aware of order and of divine*

20. Kahneman, *Thinking, Fast and Slow*, 215–17.

intangibles, and we naturally adopt the "intentional stance," thinking of God as consciously acting on us. The language may sound modern, but the insight is not unique to us today. Many a mystical thinker over the ages has understood the whole cosmos to be holy, with God as immanent within it rather than transcendent "above" it. Many a rationalist has railed against anthropomorphism (understanding God in human terms). This is not new, though the discoveries of modern science, I suggest, help us understand it, and thus God, better.

3

The Mystery of Prophecy I

Biblical Dilemmas

Joseph said to them, "Are not (dream) interpretations God's? Tell me your dreams."[1]

—GENESIS 40:8

The interpretation of dreams is the royal road to a knowledge of the unconscious activities of the mind.[2]

—SIGMUND FREUD

The Hebrew Bible is full of prophets and prophecy: from the towering figure of Moses in the Pentateuch through many others, some famous and others obscure, in the books of Joshua, Judges, Samuel, Kings and Chronicles, plus, of course, fourteen books specifically named for prophets who are their ostensible authors, and a fifteenth about, though not by, the prophet Jonah.[3] With God presented biblically as personally involved with, and talking to, many

1. Translation by author.

2. Freud, *Interpretation of Dreams*.

3. Modern scholars debate whether the works of more than one prophet are included in some of these books. Isaiah, for example, at the very least contains the works of one sixth-century-BCE prophet and one eighth-century-BCE prophet.

of these prophets, it is not enough simply to say that God is real as a creative power or principle of organization. If God is an it that does not intentionally communicate ideas, what do we make of prophecy? Certainly we cannot simply chuck this rich and profound literature and come out with anything that could still be considered Judaism. The same, for that matter, holds true for Christianity and Islam. All three religions base themselves on books which in some sense have classically been regarded by their adherents as "the word of God." The inescapable implication of God being a set of principles rather than a conscious being, however, is that God does not talk. We may, to be sure, infer the presence of the Holy and its implications for our lives from our experience of nature, of love, of art and more—and we shall return to such considerations after dealing with prophecy. But we "people of the book," as Muslims have called Jews and Christians, have so much at stake in prophecy, which many naively think of as God's dictation, that the phenomenon deserves extended attention. That is, when someone says, "Why should I not steal or commit adultery? Why should I love my neighbor as myself? Why should I eat certain foods, not eat others, and perform various rituals—saying prayers, lighting candles, reading Scripture, and so on?," if God is not a conscious personality we can no longer blithely insist, "Because God said so," providing chapter and verse for proof. We can and do still say, "Because our sacred tradition, in its deep and venerable wisdom, mandates these ethical and ritual norms"—quoting, of course, the very same verses for proof. But there is no use pretending the wisdom of previous generations carries the same weight, the same *authority*, as saying it is all directly from God.

That should not be as big a shock to moderns as it may at first sound. Nineteenth-century biblical criticism found evidence in the Torah and much of Scripture that it was stitched together and edited from multiple sources, and speculated about why this or that practice or belief entered the tradition when it did. That long ago compromised the easy conviction that every word, every commandment, came directly from God. There was a long process of authorship, editing, and changing ideas. Early on, for instance, God was presented as "visiting the guilt of the parents upon the children, upon the third and upon the fourth generations" (Exod 20:5 and Deut 5:9), and later that belief was changed: "a child shall not share the burden of a parent's guilt" (Ezek 18:20). Or again, in biblical times you were a member of the people of Israel if your father was, even if your mother was not, but in rabbinic times that was reversed. Even ethics changed. Few if any moderns would implement the commandment that "stubborn and rebellious sons" should be tried and executed (Deut 21:18–21) or that witches should be killed (Exod 22:17). Many careful readers down through the ages have noticed such inconsistencies, changes and moral quandaries, but managed to regard them as rare exceptions and thus not so significant as to shake their faith that a great deal of the Bible, if not quite all of it, literally came via prophecy from God.

Thus if we in our day, as I have suggested, are going to take philosophical God concepts—order of being or any of the others—seriously, we need to face squarely the phenomenon of prophecy. Even in biblical times prophecy was not as simple as we might think. What might the prophets of biblical times, and their contemporaries, have thought they were doing? If we are correct that God did not talk to them, why did they say God did? Those questions will persist when, in the next chapter, we take a look at how the rabbinic tradition radically reconceptualized prophecy. Then I will take a contemporary stab at accounting for what might have been going on, and how prophetic stories and literature still fit in our faith.

PROPHECY IN BIBLICAL LITERATURE

To be culturally literate in the Western world, and certainly to have grown up in a religious home, is to recognize and likely cherish uncounted prophetic passages, among them:

> I hate, I despise your feasts,
> And I will take no delight in your solemn assemblies. . . .
> But let justice roll down like waters,
> And righteousness as a mighty stream. (Amos 5:21 and 24)

> It has been told you, O man, what is good,
> And what the Lord requires of you,
> Only to do justly,
> And to love mercy,
> And to walk humbly with your God. (Mic 6:8)

> And He shall judge between the nations,
> And shall decide for many peoples;
> And they shall beat their swords into plowshares
> And their spears into pruning hooks.
> Nation shall not lift up sword against nation,
> Neither shall they learn war any more. (Isa 2:4)

> The hand of the Lord came upon me. He took me out by the spirit of the Lord and set me down in the valley. It was full of bones. He led me all around them; there were very many of them spread over the valley, and they were very dry. He said unto me, "O mortal, can these bones live again?" I replied, "O Lord God, only You know." (Ezek 37:1–3)

Consider the style as well as the memorable content. Such passages, Ezekiel's prose no less than the poetry of Amos, Micah and Isaiah, are highly
sophisticated literary creations. Readers who are not familiar with the way
biblical poetry works should note that while the lines do not rhyme, as English readers expect of classic verse, they use a device known as parallelism,
saying each thing at least twice. Thus, looking at the Amos passage, the first
two lines quoted above are not two statements but one, and the same holds
for the next two lines. In the Micah passage the first two lines are a couplet,
but the next statement is made three times. Isaiah's six lines are likewise
three couplets. The repetition creates different nuances of meaning and
feeling, and skillful poets vary the basic pattern in all sorts of ways—saying something more than twice, having the second line express the thought
negatively rather than positively, etc. Some biblical scholars have called
this poetic convention "thought rhymes" as opposed to the sound rhymes
so familiar to readers of English and many other languages. University of
California–Berkeley professor Robert Alter suggests this literary convention contributes "to the special unity and to the memorability (literal and
figurative) of the utterances, to the sense that they are an emphatic, bal-
anced and elevated kind of discourse . . ."[4] Likewise, not only the brief prose
quotation from Ezekiel above, but the entire chapter from which it comes is
one long metaphor, what we would call a "metaphysical conceit" if we found
it in John Donne or other English poets of his 16th and 17th centuries. As
with any literature, part of our pleasure as readers, and part of what makes a
given passage appeal emotionally as well as convey thoughts, is the writer's
skill at working within the rules of the literary genre of biblical poetry.

At its height there can be little doubt that, whatever else it was, prophecy was art. But the prophetic tradition, we shall see, did not begin that way.
While even early on there appears to be an assumption that God was involved
in prophecy, in any era the nature of the prophetic experience is a good deal
more complicated than simply God dictating messages to and for mortals.

To assess how we as moderns might reasonably read biblical prophetic
literature, or for that matter whether we think God speaks to people today,
we should first examine how the genre developed and what biblical audiences thought was going on. If we faithfully assume that God gave prophecy
to worthy individuals in antiquity, why—as we shall find classic rabbinic
theology insists—has the age of prophecy ceased? Or has it? If, on the other
hand, we entertain the possibility that a divine consciousness did not literally plant words, or at least ideas, in prophets' minds, why did one after
another say that God did so?

4. Alter, *Art of Biblical Poetry*, 9.

PROPHETS: FROM ECSTATICS TO
BEARERS OF DIVINE CRITIQUE

Before we find individuals of religious genius with books named for them, we find at least one and probably two previous phases, overlapping but still distinguishable. We have several memorable tales of bands of ecstatic prophets overcome by the spirit of God. They twirl and dance. They babble in ecstasy (possibly much like the phenomenon of glossolalia among certain Christian groups in our age). In chapter 11 of Numbers Moses must cope with one of the repeated outbreaks of bitter complaining among the people as they wander in the wilderness. They were discontent with the divine gift of manna, delicious though it was. They wanted the meat, fish and vegetables they had been accustomed to in Egypt (Num 11:4–9). God not only promises plenty of meat—"until it comes out of your nostrils and becomes loathsome to you!" (Num 11:19)—but decides that Moses needs help dealing with this rebellious, whining people. Moses is told to gather seventy trustworthy elders so that God may take some of the divine spirit which has rested upon him and place it on them, "and they can share the burden of the people with you" (Num 11:16–17). When Moses does so, these leaders begin to do something variously translated as "prophesied" or "spoke in ecstasy." The root is that used for prophecy (*nava*—*nun, vet, aleph*), often in a reflexive conjugation (*yitnab'oo*, Num 11:25, 26). With God's spirit on them, that is, they "spoke themselves," worked themselves up into a frenzy (which will become clearer with the next example). Neither in this case nor the next are we given any hint of significant content in their speech. Quite possibly, overcome by a sense of God's presence, they simply babbled. Only sixty-eight of the seventy actually showed up, but two who remained in camp when the group was summoned also spoke in ecstasy, alarming Joshua, who thought Moses' prerogatives were being challenged. "Are you wrought up on my account?" Moses asked when word was rushed to him. "Would that all the Lord's people were prophets, that the Lord put His spirit upon them!" (Num 11:29)

The divine spirit component is clear in that Numbers passage, but the overwhelming divine intoxication clearer in 1 Samuel 19. King Saul resolved to kill David. David fled to the prophet Samuel, who had anointed Saul as king and was destined to anoint David as well. When Saul hears of David's whereabouts:

> Saul sent messengers to seize David. They saw a band of prophets speaking in ecstasy, with Samuel standing by as their leader, and the spirit of God came upon Saul's messengers and they too

began to speak in ecstasy. When Saul was told about this, he
sent other messengers; but they too spoke in ecstasy. Saul sent
a third group of messengers; and they also spoke in ecstasy. So
he himself went to Ramah. When he came to the great cistern
at Secu, he asked, "Where are Samuel and David?" and was told
that they were at Naioth in Ramah. He was on his way there, to
Naioth in Ramah, when the spirit of God came upon him too;
and he walked on, speaking in ecstasy, until he reached Naioth
in Ramah. Then he too stripped off his clothes and he too spoke
in ecstasy before Samuel; and he lay naked all that day and all
night. That is why people say, "Is Saul too among the prophets?"
(1 Sam 19:20–24)

We can imagine how the felt presence of God might have such a powerful
impact upon people, even on a king. With whatever variations for different groups, this may well have been a cultural expectation for the region,
not only for Hebrews. In the story of Elijah's contest with the prophets of
Baal in 1 Kings 18 a band of 450 foreign prophets not only invoke Baal,
but "performed a hopping dance around the altar that had been set up"
(18:26). Later they "shouted louder and louder, and gashed themselves with
knives and spears, according to their practice, until the blood streamed
over them" (18:28).

Bands of prophets are mentioned numerous times in the Tanakh, as in
1 Kings 22. There the kings of Israel and Judah consult with four hundred of
them before going to battle. Most say what the kings want to hear, namely,
that they shall triumph. But one, Micaiah, predicts disaster, and turns out
to be correct.

For people upon whom the divine presence was believed to rest to
come to be thought of as favored by God with insight, as well, is not such a
great leap. The great Samuel, whom we just met as the anointer and defender
of kings, was sometimes called a *ro'eh*, a "seer," as he was when God revealed
to him that he was to name Saul king. First Samuel 9:9 even explains to the
reader that people who are "today" called "prophets" used to be called "seers."
King Saul wanted to pay the fee for the *ro'eh* to tell him what was destined to
happen. The prophet Amos at one point is called a *chozeh*, meaning someone
who can see the future. We can begin to see the development from ecstatics
who feel the presence of God to individuals—perhaps first from among the
ecstatic prophet bands—who receive special powers from God, whose spirit
rests upon them. Elijah, for instance, foretells a drought (1 Kgs 17:1), and
his disciple Elisha revives the dead (2 Kgs 4:34–35) as a favor to a worthy
woman—which is to say they have special influence over God or perhaps
even God-given powers.

These "preliterary" prophets (a useful term not only because they do not have books named after them, but because they give no appearance of being literary artists) we think of as notable individuals because of the vision and power which God gave them. Out of the background of the bands of ecstatics great individual men and women arose, a related but new phase in the development of prophecy. We may naively think of prophets primarily as seers, and certainly that aspect of the prophetic role persisted. But at this point the prophet as divine spokesperson emerged, adding a courageous willingness to give moral critique to society and its leaders, even its priests and royals. For the moment we shall continue with the example of Elijah, though we could as easily look at Nathan condemning David for adultery and murder (2 Sam 12:1–14), or Huldah's severe warnings against idolatry (2 Kgs 22:11–20). (With the mention of Huldah we should note that Hebrew Scriptures mention quite a few women prophets.[5])

Elijah, though providing visions of the future (including the drought mentioned above), is best known for his moral condemnation of the wicked King Ahab and his Phoenician wife, Jezebel. Their most glaring sin was theological. Ahab allowed his queen to bring prophets of Baal with her when they married, and joined her in idolatrous worship in Israel (1 Kgs 16:31–32). But Elijah risked his life to condemn specifically ethical crimes, as well. In 1 Kings 21 we read that in the northern kingdom's capital city, Samaria, a farmer named Naboth had a vineyard adjacent to the royal palace. King Ahab wanted it for a vegetable garden, and offered to purchase it for more than it was worth. "But Naboth replied, 'God forbid that I should give up to you what I have inherited from my fathers'" (1 Kgs 21:3). Ahab was so upset that he went to bed and refused to eat. Finding him pouting, Jezebel said he must act like a king, and promised to get the vineyard for him.

> So she wrote letters in Ahab's name and sealed them with his seal, and sent the letters to the elders and the nobles who lived in the same town with Naboth. In the letters she wrote as follows: "Proclaim a fast and seat Naboth at the front of the assembly. And seat two scoundrels opposite him, and let them testify against him: 'You have reviled God and king!' Then take him out and stone him to death." (1 Kgs 21:8–10)

The plot succeeded. Jezebel told Ahab to go and take possession of the vineyard, and he did so.

---

5. In addition to Huldah, women labelled prophets are Miriam in Exod 15:20, Deborah in Judg 4:4, and Noadiah in Neh 6:14. Isa 8:3 mentions but does not name a woman prophet. Joel prophecies that in future times "your sons and daughters shall prophesy" (3:1). For a fuller discussion, see McEntire, *Chorus of Prophetic Voices*, 205.

Then "the word of the Lord came to Elijah the Tishbite: 'Go down and confront King Ahab of Israel who [resides] in Samaria'" (1 Kgs 21:18). Elijah, heedless of his own safety, immediately went. "So, you have found me, my enemy!" exclaimed Ahab. Elijah proclaimed the doom of the king and his dynasty, adding grisly details: "the dogs shall devour Jezebel in the field of Jezreel," and dogs and birds shall consume the corpses of Ahab's line on the thrown (1 Kgs 21:23–24).

Note in this case that God directly revealed the content of the prophecy, telling of future events which for the most part come to pass. What is new in the historical development, however, is less the visioning of the future than the moral critique, including saying not what people want to hear (events will go well for you!) but what they hate to hear, generally that God is offended by their sins and severe punishment will follow.

As the emergence of charismatic and morally courageous individual prophets from bands of ecstatics was not a huge step, so it was a significant but not huge leap for such individuals to broaden the scope of their prophecy, addressing the character and shortcomings of ancient Hebrew society (and often of the neighbors' as well). Claiming to speak for God, they deliver not brief messages but often long condemnations of idolatry and social ills, only sometimes telling the future.

Amos, the earliest of these literary prophets, is often cited as a bridge figure in this development. While some literary prophets carried on at length about lax, insincere ritual, Amos, way back in the eighth century BCE, focused more on social and economic sin:

> Thus said the Lord:
> For three transgressions of Israel,
> For four, I will not revoke it:
> Because they sold for silver
> Those whose cause was just,
> And the needy for a pair of sandals.
> [Ah,] you who who trample the heads of the poor
> Into the dust of the ground,
> And make the humble walk a twisted course!
> Father and son go to the same girl,
> And thereby profane My holy name.
> They recline by every altar
> On garments taken in pledge,
> And drink in the House of their God
> Wine bought with fines they imposed. (Amos 2:5–8)

Importantly, in light of the history we have been sketching, when the high priest at the northern kingdom's sacrificial temple at Bethel told this southerner to take his criticism back where he came from, addressing him as a seer (*chozeh*), Amos responded:

> I am not a prophet [*navi*] and I am not a prophet's disciple. I am a cattle breeder and a tender of sycamore figs. But the Lord took me away from following the flock, and the Lord said to me, "Go prophesy to My people Israel." (Amos 7:14–15)

Amos specifically distanced himself from the then best-known styles of prophecy, from bands of ecstatics and royal court seers, and he would perform no miracles. He was not, in other words, what High Priest Amaziah and no doubt most others of the time thought of as a prophet. Rather, he claimed to have divine critique to offer officials and commoners alike. By the time this high or literary style of prophecy ran its course, cultural critique in God's name was precisely what would be expected of a prophet.

As the poet-prophet tradition developed, later prophets would cease to deny that they were prophets, signifying, I believe, that the word had changed meanings or, better, taken on an additional meaning. Prophets honored with books in the Tanakh condemn the bands of prophets and court prophets who say what people want to hear:

> They offer healing offhand
> for the wounds of My people,
> saying, "All is well, all is well,"
> when nothing is well.
> They have acted shamefully;
> They have done abhorrent things–
> yet they do not feel shame,
> and they cannot be made to blush. (Jer 6:14–15 and 8:11–12;
> and see Jer 27 and 28; Mic 3:5–7; and Ezek 13)

As we shall see, because prophets claim not simply to be overcome by the divine spirit, or to bring succinct messages to individuals, but rather to bring new knowledge from God, including prophecies of doom for those who do not repent and change their behavior, the question of which self-proclaimed prophets to follow and which to ignore becomes critical.

HOW DID GOD DELIVER THESE MESSAGES?

Imagine if God were to tell us, in our day, how to handle the most difficult political and ethical issues of the time. Should we allow abortions or not?

Should we intervene militarily in the world's political hot spots? Is any price too high to provide healthcare to all, or reverse global warming? Not that we lack for preachers who claim to know what God would have us do! But in our day most of them claim to be interpreting sacred Scriptures. When individuals claim that God has directly given them a message, most of society is apt—at best—to laugh at their naiveté. At worst we will call them charlatans, question their sanity, and even lock them up if they seem dangerous.

Those speaking unwelcome words in the name of God were in at least as much danger in biblical times. But while we tend to smirk at such prophetic claims today, we have just reviewed the development of prophets who came to be regarded as genuine spokespeople for God. Elijah, we saw, threatened the violent deaths—which later came to pass!—of Ahab and Jezebel. Many of the literary prophets threatened national destruction and exile as God's punishment for sinful biblical nations—who should change their ways before it is too late. Where did prophets receive such messages? "From God, of course," we have been taught to think—certainly a strange answer in our era when we scoff at anyone making such a claim. So it behooves us, as moderns, to dig more deeply into the biblical material on the prophetic process.

The book of Jeremiah begins with God's appearance to Jeremiah, who was destined, it says, even before conception, to become "a prophet [*navi*] concerning the nations" (Jer 1:5). Jeremiah, hearing this, proclaimed his inadequacy. "I don't know how to speak, / For I am still a boy," he said, to which God answered:

> Do not say, "I am still a boy,"
> But go wherever I send you
> And speak whatever I command you.
> Have no fear of them,
> For I am with you to deliver you
> —declares the Lord. (Jer 1:7)

Speaking for God was plainly risky business in the sixth century BCE too. Jeremiah would from time to time be threatened and imprisoned. Nations and their powerful leaders do not relish being condemned. Our major question, though, is not whether we should want the job of prophet, but how, exactly, biblical generations imagined that prophecy worked?

The prophetic call in Jeremiah 1 continues, "The Lord put out His hand and touched my mouth, and The Lord said to me: "Herewith I put My words into your mouth" (1:9). Only if one believes God has a hand can this be taken literally; it is poetic metaphor. Nonetheless, the point is clear that the prophetic message comes from God, who is assumed to have the power both to deliver messages and to protect his messengers.

A similar call goes to the first Isaiah in chapter 6. Isaiah "sees" *seraphim* (angels or mythic beasts) flying around a divine throne calling, "Holy, holy, holy! / The Lord of Hosts! / His presence fills the earth!" (Isa 6:3) As Isaiah too protests his unworthiness (neither he nor his generation have lips pure enough to speak God's words!),

> one of the seraphs flew over to me with a live coal, which he had
> taken from the altar
> with a pair of tongs. He touched it to my lips and declared,
> Now that this has touched your lips,
> Your guilt shall depart
> And your sin be purged away.
> Then I heard the voice of my Lord saying, "Whom shall I send?
> Who will go for us?"
> And I answered, "Here am I; send me." And he said, "Go, say to
> that people . . . [a message of doom]. (Isa 6:1–9)

Even more than with the Jeremiah passage, most would recognize this as impressive literary metaphor, difficult if not impossible to read as an actual event. But the message is clear: while no mortal is worthy of speaking for God, who is glorious almost beyond imagining, God selects and empowers prophets to do just that.

But how exactly did the first readers or hearers of Isaiah imagine that act of communication worked, the transcendent God giving ideas, even specific words, to a prophet? While in the Jeremiah passage God simply puts words in the prophet's mouth, in the Isaiah passage the whole experience may be regarded as happening within a vision: ". . . I beheld The Lord seated on a high and lofty throne . . ." (Isa 6:1). It comes across as a dream-like imaginative scene, an impression intensified by the skilled interweaving of vivid description in prose with speech in poetry. That picture of prophecy as vision calls to mind the more generalized account of prophecy in the book of Numbers: "When a prophet of The Lord arises among you, I make Myself known to him in a vision, I speak with him in a dream" (Num 12:6). We shall return to the context of that clear description, but nothing in the context undermines at least this one biblical author's explanation of how God could communicate with mortals. We could think of a vision as a paranormal phenomenon, an optical illusion produced by God, but it is at least as likely the waking equivalent of a sleep dream, an insight that came to mind while free-associating, "daydreaming." Dreams during sleep, of course, are a universal human phenomenon, and regularly include what seems visual to the dreamer while he or she is still asleep. Similarly, many of us have had the experience of going to sleep after worrying about or working on a specific issue and waking up during the night or the next morning with a solution. During sleep, and even during daydreaming, the imagination wanders where it will, and occasionally has a memorable thought. Religiously sensitive individuals in antiquity, troubled by thoughts of social injustice, idolatry or foreign armies rumored to be on the march, no doubt dreamed about such matters. They may have awakened with the conviction that they had encountered the Divine and come away with a picture of future doom or hope, and perhaps even specific wording to go with it. As medieval philosophers would later argue, the prophet used imagination to express the seemingly new ideas, clothing them in words and images. Importantly for our consideration of how the process might have been believed to work, the addition of the prophets' own imaginations accounts for why the style of various prophets is so disparate. Hosea does not sound much like Micah, and neither sounds remotely like Ezekiel, which they probably should if one divine mind were simply planting words in prophets' heads.

It is not difficult to imagine a prophet who believed he received divine inspiration going from place to place repeating the basic message with different words and imagery. So we need not insist that every verse in the literary prophets reflects a new dream-vision. Still, the repeated emphasis on dream-visions is telling. This was likely what biblical generations regarded as the prophetic process.

This likelihood is strengthened by repeated emphasis in the Hebrew Bible on dreams as vehicles of divine communication. Jacob dreams of a ladder or stairway linking heaven and earth, and that dream image is followed by a verbal promise (Gen 28:12–15). The cycle of Joseph stories is punctuated by dream messages which show God controlling and communicating human destiny (Gen 37:5–11; 40:4—41:32; 46:1–4). The book of Daniel portrays Babylonian ruler Nebuchadnezzar as aware that an ominous dream is significant, but unable to understand it. The wise men of Babylon could not help, but Daniel and his friends, knowing the true God, pray for Daniel to get the vision too, which he does, and interprets its meaning to Nebuchadnezzar, which Daniel can do, he says, because, "there is a God in heaven Who reveals mysteries, and He has made known to King Nebuchadnezzar what is to be at the end of days" (Dan 2; the quote 2:28). *How, then, might our biblical ancestors have thought God revealed God's will to kings, prophets or others? By giving them interpretable dream-visions!* Many examples could be added, but two from the literary prophets are of particular note. On the negative side, Jeremiah rails at length against false prophets who repeatedly proclaim, "I had a dream! I had a dream!" (Jer 23, the quote 23:25). Claiming prophetic inspiration could be that simple! More positively, when the prophet Joel projects the glorious time to come when Judah and Jerusalem will be restored to greatness, one telling detail is:

> I will pour out My spirit on all flesh;
> Your sons and daughters shall prophesy;
> Your old men shall dream dreams,
> And your young men shall see visions.
> I will even pour out My spirit
> Upon male and female slaves in those days. (Joel 3:1–2)

Recalling biblical poetics, in these verses of poetry, pouring out of spirit, prophesying and having dreams and visions are not four things, but parallel locutions which deepen and round out one concept. Dreams, visions and prophecy result when God's spirit pours forth. Joel's vision of the future here, moreover, echoes Moses' wish "that all the Lord's people were prophets, and The Lord put his spirit upon them!" (Num 11:29).

Before concluding this section and moving on to the vexing biblical issue of telling true from false prophets, we need to look at Moses and the Numbers 12 context of the prophecy-as-dream-vision. Moses is too far back historically, twelfth century BCE or so, for us to know how much his narratives are myth and how much are history. Still, according to the Torah it is in Moses' time that we first see ecstatic prophecy, though Moses nowhere appears to be an ecstatic himself. When in Numbers 12 his brother and sister, Aaron and Miriam, sense political vulnerability in him because he has married a Cushite woman, an outsider, they protest that God has spoken not only through Moses, but through them as well. God is furious at this challenge to the chosen leader, and this is the place where we are told—in God's name—that prophecy comes through dreams and visions, except in the case of Moses. "With him I speak mouth to mouth, plainly and not in riddles, and he beholds the likeness of The Lord" (Num 12:6–7). It would only be a slight exaggeration to read this as saying that Moses is not a prophet, at least by the standards of his time, but something higher or better. (Recall Amos insisting he is not a prophet or prophet's disciple, but a spokesperson for God.) When playing leadership roles, Aaron in Exodus 7:1 and Miriam in Exodus 15:20 have already been called prophets. What Aaron and Miriam want now is power, authority. Moses' prophecy is of a different order than anyone else's, as will be made explicit at the very end of the Torah:

> Never again did there arise in Israel a prophet like Moses—
> whom The Lord singled out face to face, for the various signs
> and portents that The Lord sent him to display in the land of
> Egypt, against Pharaoh and all his courtiers and his whole

country, and for the great might and awesome power that Moses
displayed before all Israel. (Deut 34:10–12)

Many biblical scholars regard Deuteronomy as a later book, sixth century
BCE, by which time we are at the height of literary prophecy. Perhaps the
notion that Moses was a prophet was read back into earlier incidents by later
generations with a different understanding of prophecy. Even if we regard
Moses as a prophet throughout his career, he is, again, a prophet of a different order altogether, not a literary artist with a social critique, though
still a deliverer of insight from God. We are entitled to a healthy skepticism
about prophetic claimants other than Moses, for none of them share Moses'
distinction of receiving prophecy "face to face,"[6] and dreams are open to
interpretation.

Summing up this section, the biblical audience could understand
dreams and visions as the medium of prophetic communication. Some may
even have understood Moses' revelations that way, for another Mosaic narrative says Moses was denied when he requested to see God's face, for "you
cannot see My face, for man may not see My face and live" (Exod 33:17–23,
quote is in 33:20). Even for Moses the "face to face" image may well be pure
metaphor, expressing Moses' intimate relationship with the divine. When
anyone else claimed prophecy, the biblical generations presumably heard a
claim of divinely inspired dream-visions.

COULD PROPHETS' CONTEMPORARIES
BE ANY SURER THAN WE MODERNS
THAT GOD WAS SPEAKING?

The claim of a dream or vision left ample room for skepticism even in antiquity. Then as now, presumably everyone had dreams, but apparently only a
few thought they were divine communications. That perception must have
been based on their reaction to the content. Even when the dream seemed
significant, some were perplexed by content they could not understand (as
in the Joseph story and the book of Daniel), and others reacted with overwhelming ecstasy at the divine glory—numinous, effulgent, so grand that
first Moses and later the people at Sinai feared to see it themselves (Exod 3:6
and 20:15–18; Deut 5:5). Since everyone had dreams, ordinary ones at least,
prophets could be commoners or important people—or might be fake! A

6. In Gen 32 the patriarch Jacob wrestles with a mysterious person in the dark
(32:25), later called God (32:31), but does not receive a prophetic message. In Exod 24
Moses, Aaron, Nadab, Abihu and seventy elders see God on Sinai (24:11), but then only
Moses goes on to the top of the mountain to receive the commandments.

given dream might be recognized as extraordinary, a seeming revelation for individuals or for the whole nation, or not, but the medium itself would have seemed credible to anyone who understood at least some dreams as from God.

What is believable today? In our time dreams are regarded as windows on the subconscious mind. There is no proof, of course, that a personal God does not plant dreams in our heads, or at least in prophets' heads. But in an era when our thinking is shaped by the scientific worldview and method, the burden of proof lies with those who claim to have received a message from God. Any dream could be ephemeral and of no real significance, or, for that matter, evidence of psychosis.

That biblical generations believed God communicated with mortals is beyond doubt. But they too had their doubts about specific claimants to the mantle of prophecy. As we have seen, anyone could say, "I've had a dream! I've had a dream!" based on which one ought to go forth to battle, reorder society in pursuit of compassion and justice, stop bringing second rate animals for sacrifice or cease sacrificing altogether! When prophetic claimants were on both sides of any significant question (like political pundits or stock market tipsters today), what was one to do?

Deuteronomy 18 promises God will send the people genuine prophets, but warns against imitating any individual who "consigns his son or daughter to the fire, or who is an augur, a soothsayer, a diviner, a sorcerer, one who casts spells, or one who consults ghosts or familiar spirits, or one who inquires of the dead," for such practices of neighboring peoples are "abhorrent to the Lord" (18:9–11). Even Hebrews may lead the people astray:

> I will raise up a prophet for them from among their own people, like yourself [Moses]: I will put My words in his mouth and he will speak to them all that I command him; and if anybody fails to heed the words he speaks in My name, I Myself will call him to account. But the prophet who presumes to speak in My name an oracle which I did not command him to utter, or to speak in the name of other gods—that prophet shall die. And should you ask yourselves, "How can we know that the oracle was not spoken by The Lord?"—if the prophet speaks in the name of the Lord and the oracle does not come true, that oracle was not spoken by The Lord; the prophet has spoken it presumptuously: do not stand in dread of him. (Deut 18:18–22; see also 13:1–19)

The logic, of course, is both unassailable and useless! If a prophet, for instance, says you must cease—or begin—a certain behavior or you will be destroyed, you cannot wait to find out if the oracle comes true to decide if it is genuine, since that will be too late. Still, such passages demonstrate that the institution of prophecy was respected by both Hebrews and their neighbors, and that the danger of false prophecy was recognized. Jeremiah, with perhaps unintended irony, also helps a bit, averring that in the past prophets have generally prophesied "war, disease, disaster and pestilence. . . . So if a prophet prophesies good fortune, then only when the word of the prophet comes true can it be known that The Lord really sent him" (Jer 28:8–9).

Were there really so many "false prophets"? Apparently so, else Jeremiah would not be proclaiming:

> For from the smallest to the greatest,
> They are greedy for gain;
> Priest and prophet alike,
> They all act falsely.
> They offer healing offhand
> For the wounds of My people,
> Saying, "All is well, all is well,"
> When nothing is well.
> They have acted shamefully;
> They have done abhorrent things—
> Yet they do not feel shame,
> And they cannot be made to blush . . . .
> (Jer 6:13–14; and see 8:8–12; 2:8; 23:9–40, and the narrative about false prophet Hananiah in Jer 28)

Neither, if such cases were unknown, would Micah condemn court prophets who "divine for pay" and are thus no different from corrupt judges and priests (Mic 3:5–12, especially 3:11). Zechariah likewise proclaims that false prophets will die—put to death by their own parents!—for their lies (Zech 13:2–6). And Ezekiel 13 goes on at length condemning those who "prophesy out of their own imagination: Hear the word of The Lord!" (Ezek 13:3)

So it is scarcely new that we question the veracity and even worry about the sanity of those who claim God talks to them. The biblical connection of prophecy to dream-visions is no help for moderns. Our brains, medical science has learned, do not cease to process thoughts during sleep. Particularly during REM sleep[7] people have dreams, often vivid dreams related to events and concerns in our lives. Dreams may often be windows on the workings of our unconscious minds. We may learn from them or experience creative breakthroughs from them. Yet as we have learned more

---

7. People generally cycle into deeper and shallower sleep several times in a given night. The phase of the sleep cycle when we do most of our dreaming is REM (for "rapid eye movement") sleep, during which researchers have found that association of ideas and thus creativity are enhanced.

and more about dreams and interpreting dreams we have become less and less likely to see them as messages from God. We generate them ourselves. The biblical approach is not inconceivable in the case of any particular dream, but more likely explanations are at hand. So if one among many dreams were from God, how would we know which one? And might some dreams be demonic? The biblical assumption that dreams are from God and thus can guide us to do God's will was problematic in its time, and even less compelling today.

4

The Mystery of Prophecy II

Postbiblical Perspectives

We have only one mind. When we dream, one part is developing a sequence of hallucinated scenes, and another part is making them fit together in a story. . . . The dream is hallucinated, but not everything in it is imaginary. If you hear a car alarm in your dream, it might be hallucinated—or a car alarm might actually be howling in the streets.[1]

—DAVID GALERNTER

We have seen that biblical generations assumed God would want to give them guidance, and thus would send prophets to instruct them (Deut 18:18)—only to find that it was extraordinarily difficult to know which prophetic claimants to heed. Talmudic authorities, early rabbinic sages, had similar problems. They solved them by saying, contrary to Deuteronomy 18:18, that God was no longer sending prophets! Why not? The stated reason was that the children of Israel, with many of them no longer living in the land of Israel, had become unworthy. When the Babylonian exile ended, a large number did not return to *eretz yisrael* even though they could have done so. Thus, according to the Talmud, after the latest prophets, Haggai, Zechariah and Malachi, God

---

1. Galernter, *Tides of Mind*, 197.

simply stopped giving such revelations. Occasionally a rabbinic sage might hear a weaker form of verbal revelation, a sort of echo of the divine voice known as the *Bat Kol* ("daughter of a Voice"), but the age of full-strength prophecy was over (*b. Yoma* 9b). God no longer worked that way.

Why? Did God's people no longer need guidance? The real problem here was the unpredictability of what any given individual might say is the word of God. The institution of prophecy is inherently destabilizing. Imagine: beliefs and practices are what they are, and then someone comes along and says they must be changed. Established authorities (priests and kings in biblical times; priests early on, and civil authorities, then rabbis and other religious leaders in Talmudic times), no doubt felt threatened. "Who are you to say we are doing things wrong?" leaders ask. "God sent me to tell you!" the self-proclaimed prophet responds. That is a discussion stopper if ever there was one! So the early rabbis, who saw their authority as resting not on their ability to receive more scripture directly, but on their ability to interpret Scripture, insisted that God had already given a complete Torah, so further prophecy would be superfluous.[2] Who were its proper interpreters? The rabbis themselves, of course! Priests and government officials, though, would have been even less inclined to give credence to those regarded by themselves or others as new prophets, for while the Temple still stood these officials were more "the establishment" than the rabbis.[3]

With a decisive push from the Romans, who destroyed the Jerusalem Temple in the year 70 CE, the priesthood dramatically declined. Intellectual leadership was difficult to determine even before the destruction, with priests and rabbis, Pharisees, Sadducees, Essenes and other splinter groups vying, Hellenistic thought widespread in Roman realms, Gnostics, and early Kabbala and more. We cannot simply say that the Temple disappeared and the rabbis took over, for that took several centuries. Still, for prophecy as for much else, it is a reasonable generalization to say that when the smoke finally cleared, rabbinic thought dominated. The rabbis, a new, postbiblical set of religious teachers, gradually established their authority. They left literary records in the form of Mishnah (a law code developed during the first two centuries CE), Gemarrah (a commentary on the Mishnah, third through

---

2. This is a slight simplification, for the interpretations came to be regarded as more Torah, though this "Oral Torah" remained flexible until it had to be written down for fear it would be lost under Roman oppression. Nevertheless, the Tanakh, which was believed to have come from God through prophets, continued to be regarded as a higher form of revelation, and further prophecy was over.

3. In this sense New Testament accounts of the hostile reaction of some Jews to Jesus, who is called prophet as well as Messiah, ring true. For Jesus called prophet see, for instance, Matt 21:10–11; Mark 6:15; Luke 7:16; John 6:14.

sixth century CE, studied with and later printed together with the Mishnah to together comprise the Talmud), and various other texts, of particular note collections of commentaries, sayings and stories known as midrash.

The tractate (or chapter) of the Mishnah regarded as a sort of foundation for the rest, *Avot*, begins by downplaying the prophets. As the rabbis conceptualized, and Jews print, Bibles, the "five Books of Moses," or Torah, come first, leading on to the longest section, the Prophets (first histories with prophets included, the books of Joshua, Judges, Samuel and Kings, then the books named for their prophetic authors). After Torah and Prophets the Hebrew Bible ends with a grab bag of everything left, various "Writings." So Moses came first, then later prophets. The rabbis did not change that order, but they not-so-subtly called Moses *Moshe Rabbenu*, "Moses our *Rabbi*." Furthermore—*m. Avot* 1:1—they say that "Moses received Torah at Sinai, and transmitted it to Joshua, and Joshua to the elders, and the elders to the prophets, and the prophets transmitted it to the men of the Great Assembly . . ." Suddenly, *Avot* asserts, the prophets' importance is as transmitters of the tradition, not originators or innovators! The men of the Great Assembly may have been scholars, learned in Torah like rabbis, who saw their task—the rest of the *Avot* 1:1 passage—as to "be deliberate in judgement, raise up many disciples, and build a fence around the Torah." The links in the middle of the chain of tradition are worthy of honor, but the sacred endeavor, bringing divine wisdom to the people, has been reconceptualized. It leads from a rabbi to rabbis, the latter of whom should be careful expounders and protectors (building a metaphorical fence, not a literal one, to prevent accidental violation) of Torah.

In the same context, moreover, note the teaching is that "Moses received Torah," not ". . . *the* Torah." *The* Torah in Jewish parlance was and is the Pentateuch, the first five books of the Tanakh, regarded as Mosaic though Moses had not yet been born in Genesis and dies a bit before the end of Deuteronomy. "Torah" generically, as opposed to "*the* Torah," means sacred teaching: the entire Tanakh, Talmud, Midrash and the "tree" of rabbinic literature rooted in the Bible and thus possessing Sinaitic authority if carefully—rabbinically—interpreted. As a midrash puts it:

> When God revealed Himself at Sinai to give the Torah to Israel, He communicated it to Moses in order: Bible, Mishnah, Talmud and Haggadah, as it says, And God spoke all these words (Exod 20:1). Even the question a pupil asks his teacher God told Moses at that time. After he had learnt it from God, He told him to teach it to Israel. (*Midr. Rab., Exod. Rab.* 47:1)

At first glance, one wonders how forty days and forty nights on Sinai could have been enough for all the revelation Moses was thought to have received! But of course the length is not the issue here, but rather the idea that properly interpreted Scripture comes with Sinaitic—*divine*—authority. If mortals with finite minds—the likes of Homer, Shakespeare and other greats—can write texts with multiple layers of meaning, surely God, conceived as having an infinite mind, can put meanings for future as well as current generations into texts, an infinite number of hints awaiting the elucidation of interpreters down through the ages. Another midrash reports that "Not only did all the prophets receive their prophecy from Sinai, but also each of the sages in every generation received his [wisdom] from Sinai . . ." (*Midr. Rab., Exod. Rab.* 28:6).

Rabbinic interpretations of Torah, it was believed, were implicit in the original. In the first paragraph of this chapter we noted the Talmud's assertion that prophecy had ceased (*b. Yoma* 9b). Talmud *b. Shab.* 104a even more pointedly says that prophets had never introduced anything new to Torah, citing Leviticus 27:34, "These are the commandments (that the Lord commanded the children of Israel at Mount Sinai)" as a proof text. "These are the commandments"—with none further needed! The Torah is complete. Prophets, we might say, were great preachers, fine interpreters, but God revealed nothing to them that was not already in the Torah. When guidance is needed, then, look not for a convincing prophet, but for a knowledgeable rabbi skilled at interpreting Torah to apply it to new situations.

That must have been a comfortable conviction for rabbis struggling to adapt Judaism to a post-Temple world. It not only minimized the danger from new prophetic claimants, but also left them, as scholars of Torah, the authoritative interpreters of God's will. But I ask you to buckle your seatbelts for a quick flight over the next couple of thousand years. At the time of the earliest rabbis, the first century CE, Christianity came along. The church would claim it had a "New Testament," a further revelation from the same and only God, which mandated changes in beliefs and practices. This may have further provided incentive to the early rabbis to declare that the age of prophecy was past.[4] By the end of the second century, though, once their religion was launched, early Christians too insisted that the age of prophecy was past.[5] Then in the sixth century a prophet in the Arabian peninsula, Moham-

---

4. Rabinowitz, "Prophets and Prophecy," 1176.

5. Mitchell, "Prophecy (Christian)," 383–84. Also see Sheppard and Hebrechtsmeier, "Prophecy: An Overview," 11. The authors of the latter observe: "As the words of these historical prophets attained reverential status within scriptural canons, the book replaced the living religious specialist as the primary agent of revelational mediation. The history of surviving religious traditions with a prophetic Scripture (now Judaism,

med, aware of Judaism and Christianity, claimed that Jews and Christians both had authentic prophets, but that God dictated a further revelation, section by section, to him. Mohammed's followers too, in relatively short order, announced that Mohammed was not only the greatest prophet, but also "the seal of the prophets," the last, a decision necessitated by the competing claims to revelation of other Arab tribal leaders.[6] Again, there was nothing more to be said. Do not tell that, though, to the followers of Joseph Smith and the Church of Jesus Christ of Latter-Say Saints in nineteenth-century America. But Smith's revelation, they said, was the final one!

There is no mistaking the pattern. Prophets—true, false, naïve, characterize them as we may—had a habit of saying things people did not want to hear, and challenging established orders. For those who believe literally in divine revelation via prophecy, the question is how religion after religion presumes to limit God's right or ability to give further prophecy. And what, beyond filial piety, makes any of us think that the God of all would communicate more with our tribe than others'? To be sure, classical Reform Judaism spoke of "progressive revelation," praying that "we may see and welcome all truth, whether shining from the annals of ancient revelations or reaching us through the seers of our own time; for Thou hidest not Thy light from any generation of Thy children that feel after Thee and seek Thy guidance."[7] This abstract universalism, however, has not been translated into a list of examples of postbiblical prophets (Hillel? Herzl? M. L. King Jr.?), or even a statement that we would be obligated to follow their teachings if we recognized some.

Summing up what we have seen thus far, prophecy was a widely recognized though not always respected phenomenon in biblical times. But the age of prophecy ended. Postbiblically, prophecy became, at most, rare. We cannot prove that God's spirit never overwhelmed whole bands of ecstatics, or that God never spoke at length with individuals, sending them to spread word of divine displeasure with Israel's faithlessness and moral decay, replete with warnings and promises depending upon whether the message was taken to heart. Well over two thousand years later there are still, as we shall see, people who claim to hear the voice of God. Few of them, however, claim to be prophets, and those who do are regarded with suspicion. Naturalistic explanations of the biblical phenomenon and its modern echoes help to clear up the mystery. But of course they also challenge the religious among us to find other evidence of God's reality in our lives.

Christianity and Islam) has depended in no small measure upon this development."

6. Waldman, "Nubuwah," 3.

7. *Union Prayerbook*, 39.

A MODERN DEFENSE OF A
TRADITIONALIST UNDERSTANDING

Theologian Abraham Joshua Heschel struggled mightily in his book *The Prophets* to refute nineteenth- and early-twentieth-century Bible critics who accounted for prophecy naturalistically as opposed to supernaturalistically. A learned and gifted writer and the descendent of Hasidic masters, Heschel can be regarded as a bridge figure between traditionalism and modernism, having received an Orthodox education in his native Poland before going to Germany to earn a modern PhD (*The Prophets* began as his doctoral dissertation, though it was expanded in the English edition). One can scarcely imagine a better defender of traditional ideas of prophecy. For Heschel, God simply had to be actively involved in the prophetic process, and he argued against the idea that such tropes as "Thus saith the Lord" could simply be literary devices to give the ideas weight, or that the prophecies could be products of the unconscious workings of the prophets' minds.[8] Maimonides centuries earlier envisioned the prophets—naturalistically— developing their intellects to the point that they could virtually think God's thoughts with God,[9] so that there would be no need for God to interrupt the natural order by placing words or ideas in prophets' heads. Modern critics suggested that prophecies were entirely the product of the prophets' own minds. Heschel, to the contrary, stressed that the prophets were partners with the divine, sharing God's emotion, God's "pathos."[10] Maimonides and other Aristotelians would have been shocked at the idea that God had emotions at all, though the literary prophets themselves, who spoke regularly of God's love and anger, might well have agreed.

Heschel also challenges moderns with the fact that prophets like Isaiah not only claimed to have heard God, but condemned others for falsely making that claim. That would have been hypocritical had they not believed they themselves had truly heard God. Would we call Isaiah a liar?![11] "That the prophets themselves were convinced of the divine origin of their pronouncements is beyond dispute," Heschel insists. But even he must ultimately admit:

8. Heschel, *Prophets*. See especially chapters 22–24. For prophecy as a "literary device" in particular, see pp. 414–15.

9. Maimonides, *Guide for the Perplexed*, 225–27.

10. Heschel, *Prophets*, 26: "An analysis of prophetic utterances shows that the fundamental experience of the prophet is a fellowship with the feelings of God, a *sympathy with the divine pathos*, a communion with the divine consciousness which comes about through the prophet's reflection of, or participation in, the divine pathos." (Emphasis original)

11. Heschel, *Prophets*, 416–17.

It is not within our power to decide about the nature of the visions and voices perceived by the prophets: whether they were
real or merely subjective phenomena; whether the voice was
perceived in trance or in a waking state. It is vain to speculate
how the divine mind coalesces with the human, or to ask at
what point the divine begins to operate; whether the formula
"thus says the Lord" introduced a verbally inspired message; or
whether only the thought was revealed, the language being the
prophet's own.[12]

I concur that the prophets were not knowingly lying, but I suggest they may
well have been fooled by their own mindset, their paradigm of how God and
religion work, and by their lack of awareness—thousands of years ago—that
more goes on subconsciously than consciously in each of our brains.

Verbal revelation through prophecy, then, though it can be believed
as an article of faith, is neither demonstrable nor refutable. Prophecy has
always presented both practical and logical problems, even to the point that
postbiblical Judaism, followed by Christianity and Islam, denied that there
would be more of it. Yet here we are, heirs to magnificent, inspiring prophetic literature which we are loathe to discard. If modern thought, as we
have seen, challenges our faith in prophecy and thus Scripture as the literal
word of God, might modern thought clarify what did go on in prophecy?
How could the prophets have been so convinced they were speaking for
God if the ideas arose in their own heads?

MULTIPLE VOICES IN OUR BRAINS

Our brains work very differently from computers. Nevertheless, they are, in
part, information processors, so computer metaphors can be helpful. Like a
computer, your brain runs multiple "programs" at once. It has sensory programs receiving and analyzing what you see, touch, smell, and so on. It has
programs monitoring activity in the rest of your body determining when you
are hungry, thirsty, tired, in pain, feeling lusty, etc. It has thought programs
to analyze your current situation, others to think abstractly and still others to
plan your day or your career. These are memory modules, pattern recognition modules, emotional programs governing how you react, etc., etc., etc.
The wonder is that all this comes together and you move along reasonably
smoothly through life. But there is no separate "you" spot in your brain where
all this comes together. You are the sum total of all these working together and,
indeed, competing with one another moment by moment for dominance.

12. Heschel, *Prophets*, 429.

Imagine you are reading when suddenly you hear a snake hissing nearby. An immediate emotional reaction takes over; the reading can wait! Or you are reading and your spouse calls you for dinner. This time you may finish the sentence or even the page—unless of course you are really hungry! Again, all these programs are going at once, competing for momentary dominance. Borrowing a phrase from historian Doris Kearns Goodwin's book on Abraham Lincoln's cabinet, neuroscientist David Eagleman writes, "I propose that the brain is best understood as a team of rivals." The brain, like Lincoln's cabinet, contains competing factions, united, nevertheless, by the common goal of the survival and thriving of the organism (body for you and me, body politic for the cabinet).[13] If you have been angry enough to want to punch someone in the nose, or to tell a shameful secret that will destroy the antagonist's reputation, you will likely recall an interior dialogue something like this: "It will serve him right!" "Yes, but do I want to be responsible for that?" "If I get into trouble, will it have been worth it? Is it really that big a deal?" "Big enough; so what should I do?!" Most any temptation to violate a law or cultural norm (theft, adultery, even going off your diet) provokes such a cascade of competing "voices" in your head. This is not a matter of mental illness, but of routine brain functioning. The whole system somehow reaches a conclusion, emotion sometimes instantly trumping more rational considerations, but more critical thinking programs more often holding passion in check.

The nature of consciousness is relevant to any speculation about biblical prophecy. We all dream, but mostly forget our dreams. If we make a point of remembering them, however, or when occasionally they frighten or thrill us, we may recall them. Prophets would have too. We get excited about ideas we develop when awake as well. Some prophetic visions, understood naturalistically, may have been ideas that sprang to mind as a prophet mulled something over, or simply "daydreamed." Greek mathematician Archimedes is said to have been troubled by the question of how one could know how much water was displaced when an object was submerged in it. Legend has it that one day he stepped into a bath and noticed that the water level rose. "Eureka! Eureka! (I have found it!)" he exclaimed. The volume displaced, he realized, must be equal to the volume of what is put in the water. If we think about it, though, Archimedes' sudden realization was not actually so sudden. He had been thinking about the problem without finding the answer until a new bit of data, or a new way of looking at the data, came to mind. Various artists speak of whole melodies or poems virtually writing themselves. They are not writing

13. Eagleman, *Incognito*, 108–9.

themselves, of course, but are the work of well trained and experienced minds, though the breakthrough happens at a subconscious level.[14] More analytical brain programs tend to explain experience based on previous experience, and to censor what seems incongruous or impossible. That function diminishes during daydreaming and free-associating, and is largely turned off, as it were, during sleep. At such times a prophet or creative artist—or any of us!—may put ideas together that would otherwise be censored or changed to match familiar understandings.[15] We can speculate that if the new though pattern solves a problem we have been mulling over, we may be fortunate enough to remember it. (If you wake up with an insight, you are well advised to write it down before it can recede from consciousness!) Similarly, an artist might unconsciously come up with a new image, story or melody this way.

Now imagine a world in which it was believed that dreams and daydreams were not from the unconscious mind—a concept not to be discovered for centuries—but from *God* (or gods). Assyriologist and biblical critic Tikva Frymer-Kensky reports messages were believed to come from gods through dreams at least as far back as 2200 BCE, and that there was a developed process in Mesopotamia for "incubating" and then interpreting dreams.[16] Hebrews, correctly, did not see themselves as unique in turning to dream-diviners. Emperor Nebuchadnezzar calls for them in Daniel 4:4. Moabite king Balak calls for Moabite and Midianite diviners when concerned about what to do with the Israelites crossing his territory. They go to

14. Two examples: On a coach ride from Boston to Washington, D.C. as the American Civil War was beginning in 1861, poet Julia Ward Howe was humming the song she had heard troops in Boston singing, "John Brown's Body," and a fellow rider suggested, "Why don't you write some good words for that tune?" She slept soundly that night, she reported, "and as I lay waiting for the dawn, the long lines of the poem began to twine themselves" together in her head. She arose to write them down before forgetting them. She reported that it seemed "as if they came to her in a revelation." With the change of only four words from the first draft, it was to be "The Battle Hymn of the Republic." See Tharp, "Song That Wrote Itself." A better-known example is Samuel Taylor Coleridge's waking one morning in 1797 to write "Kubla Kahn; or, A Vision in a Dream: A Fragment," though Coleridge had the further help of a dose of opium. He reported not finishing the poem because of an hour's interruption while he was writing, after which he could not remember the rest. See Abrams, "Kubla Khan," 197–98.

15. Damasio, *Self Comes to Mind*, 178, discusses "mind process unassisted by consciousness." Gazzaniga, *Human*, 292–95 and 300–301, goes so far as to suggest that the left-brain interpretive function of putting all our perceptions into one narrative is what gives us the illusion of being a single consciousness, not a "team." Linden, *Accidental Mind*, 215, notes explicitly that portions of the prefrontal cortex responsible for judgement, logic, planning . . . and working memory" are deactivated during REM sleep, perhaps contributing to the illogical nature of dreams and our willingness to believe them.

16. Frymer-Kensky, *In the Wake of the Goddesses*, 38.

the Moabite prophet Balaam, who has them stay the night so he can receive his revelation before answering Balak's invitation to come and curse Israel (Num 22:7–8). The process is repeated when a second group of emissaries arrives (Num 22:18–19). Balaam almost certainly needed a dream, not just darkness, to know God's will!

But did new knowledge have to come at night? The Greeks, similarly, had nine goddesses, the muses, for inspiration, and biblically we have seen that God gave prophecy in dreams and visions, the latter of which could be daydreams. Where you or I, or Coleridge or Archimedes, would think we had a dream or sudden insight, so that the new idea or creation felt like our own, could not Malachi or Jeremiah have thought they had divine visitations?

A simpler but only partial explanation is available for starters. A prophet who genuinely believed he or she received a dream or daydream message from God would preach it. When ignored or condemned, the prophet probably repeated it, perhaps many times, likely elaborating with further metaphors and different wording to get the idea across. The prophet did not need a new dream to introduce the old message as God's. *"Thus saith the Lord," "The word of God," and such phrases were quite possibly a literary convention involving no deceit.* Especially from a dream, the message, not the exact phrasing, was of the essence. In our culture when I begin a story, "Once upon a time such-and-such happened," though I have literally said something occurred, thanks to a well-established literary convention you understand that the story is fiction. Literary conventions matter. Heschel is right, though, that it would be hypocritical for prophets to condemn others for doing what they themselves were knowingly doing. I concur: we do not want to call Isaiah a liar! So without literary exaggeration, conscious deceit or mental illness, is there any possibility that at least some of the prophets, on some occasions, not only when asleep but also when awake, truly believed they heard the voice of God?

The notion of the brain operating as a "team of rivals" is not controversial in today's cognitive studies. As you hear inner "voices" and feel conflicting emotions, some of which you speak, write or act upon and more of which you probably do not, so, no doubt, did religiously motivated and morally obsessed prophets. To modern cognitive studies that is no longer mysterious. What we still need, however, is some mechanism for the prophets thinking they literally heard what was actually internally generated, and to that challenge we turn next.

SOME PSYCHOLOGY, SOME ANTHROPOLOGY

So let us become more speculative in pursuit of the mystery of prophecy. In 1976, a long time ago in terms of the revolution occurring in cognitive studies and neuroscience, a Princeton psychologist named Julian Jaynes wrote a book with the descriptive but intimidating title, *The Origin of Consciousness in the Breakdown of the Bicameral Mind.* I had heard nothing of it for years, but recently I have found references to it popping up, including in Eagleman's book *Incognito*, referred to above for its metaphor of the brain as a "team of rivals."[17] The right and left hemispheres of the human brain are so much alike that if someone, prior to her eighth birthday, must have the left or right hemisphere surgically removed, she can go on to lead a normal life. In human evolution, Jaynes proposed, about three millennia ago the left hemisphere of the brain essentially took orders from the right—orders that it heard as commands from the gods. People did no rational analysis (which is today predominantly a left-brain function) and thus had no "introspective consciousness."[18] Counterintuitive though this is for us today, people did not have the sort of interior dialogue sketched above in which we question our own motives, values and interests in deciding on a course of action. Based on its conditioning and situation, the right brain indicated to the left what action to take. The person—or her left brain—literally heard, Jaynes insists, and thus believed an unseen presence, a god, was giving orders. Some three thousand years ago the two hemispheres of the brain began to communicate better, allowing more influence to the left hemisphere and, in the process, introspection and consciousness.

The three phases of prophecy we discussed in the previous chapter cover roughly 1200 BCE to 500 BCE, as the evolution from left brain hearing right brain as the voice(s) of gods or God was gradually ending and self-consciousness growing. What Jaynes calls "the origin of consciousness" coincided with the growth of prophecy. More bluntly: prophets truly heard voices. But the voices came from within. Consider Jaynes's analysis of Amos, the first literary prophet:

> In Amos there are no words for mind or think or feel or understand or anything similar whatever; Amos never ponders anything in his heart; he can't; he would not know what it meant. In the few times he refers to himself, he is abrupt and informative without qualification; he is no prophet, but a mere "gatherer of sycamore fruit"; he does not consciously think before he speaks;

17. Eagleman, *Incognito*, 124–25.
18. Jaynes, *Origin of Consciousness*, 72–74.

in fact, he does not think at all; his thought is done for him. He feels his bicameral voice about to speak and shushes those about him with a "Thus speaks the Lord!" and follows with an angry forceful speech which he probably does not understand himself.[19]

I remain skeptical. Jaynes neglects to note that this illiterate prophet speaks in highly literary, poetic form. Why would his right brain have insights which his left brain could not appreciate but which that right brain somehow imagines are worth trying to communicate to others? Still, Jaynes's chapter devoted to biblical readings in which "bicameral voices" speak, including this observation of Amos's lack of self-awareness, is provocative.[20] He finds this bicameral phenomenon in other ancient literature as well. He insists that the voices heard in ancient tales of individuals interacting with their presumed gods are very different from the bullying voices which schizophrenics hear.[21] Still, normal people today sometimes hear voices when in stressful situations, which to Jaynes demonstrates the bicameral right-brain voice is still there. The bicameral voice and the schizophrenic voice both have their origins in stress.[22] "No one yet knows whether Jaynes's theory has legs, but the proposal is too interesting to ignore," Eagleman concludes.[23] Surely it is relevant that in ancient times people may routinely have heard such voices more than we do. If they were inclined to believe they were the voices of divine beings, they may have been naive, but they were not willfully misleading themselves or others.

The research of Tanya Luhrmann is far less speculative. A psychological anthropologist at Stanford University, she became interested in contemporary Evangelical Christianity. First in the Chicago area and later in California near Stanford University, she began visiting and participating in Evangelical churches, where she asked people if she could interview them about their religious experience. She found a much more personal theology and praxis than she knew from mainline Protestant churches. In her book *When God Talks Back*, she writes:

> One of the first things a person must master at a church like the Vineyard is to recognize when God is present and when he responds. This can seem odd to one raised in a mainstream church, where God is usually not imagined as a person with

19. Jaynes, *Origin of Consciousness*, 296.
20. Jaynes, *Origin of Consciousness*, 293–313.
21. Jaynes, Origin of Consciousness, 88–89.
22. Jaynes, Origin of Consciousness, 92.
23. Eagleman, *Incongnito*, 125.

whom you may have back-and-forth conversation throughout the day. At the Vineyard, people speak about recognizing God's "voice." They talk about things God has "said" to them . . .[24]

The style of the music and other prayers, the way the Scriptures are taught not as ancient documents from which we may derive significant insights but as God's loving guidance to each individual today, and the embracing community are all part of the experience. Since the 1960s (Luhrmann sees the roots in the hippy counterculture[25]) this style of church has burgeoned. There are some ninety to a hundred million Evangelicals in America today.[26] The significant point here is that adherents learn to listen for God speaking within their minds. In her interviewing, Luhrmann realized that many hear what they take to be God's voice outside their minds. In a *New York Times* op-ed piece based on the book, she recounted that she was doing research to better understand the growing phenomenon of charismatic Evangelical churches. Though she knew people in such churches "sought an intimate, conversational relationship with God," she was shocked when a young woman reported God had told her not to take a job she had interviewed for. The woman had looked around, but no one was there. Another time she felt God had spoken audibly from the back seat of her car. So the professor began asking all the church members she interviewed if they had ever literally heard God speak? Many believed God had told them, audibly, things like "Sit and listen" or "I will always be with you."[27]

Luhrmann's research indicated as many as a third of Evangelicals believe they have heard, with their ears, the voice of God giving them brief bits of advice—to become a minister, start a school, do one thing or not do another.[28] A third of 90–100 million people can scarcely be dismissed as mentally ill!

Luhrmann's explanation is that people in these churches have their minds trained (really retrained). While still toddlers, people develop a theory of mind in which we distinguish between our own inner thoughts, which are private and only directly known by us, and our surmise about the thoughts of others, which we infer from the situation and from visual and verbal cues ("She is angry at me"; "He is about to kiss me"; "They don't

---

24. Luhrmann, *When God Talks Back*, 39.

25. Luhrmann, *When God Talks Back*, 14–38.

26. Pew Forum, "Religious Landscape Study."

27. Lurhmann, "Is That God Talking?"

28. A Texas Evangelical pastor of my acquaintance, who has served many large churches, hearing my report of this at a clergy group, asked, "What was that number?" "A third," I responded. "Higher!" he said.

know what is going on"). To become a Christian of this stripe, Luhrmann suggests, people must learn to override basic features of theory of mind: that minds are private (God knows them), that personal entities are visible (God is not) and that "love is conditional and contingent upon right behavior (God's love is unconditional)."[29] "This new Christian theory of mind—we could call it a 'participatory' theory of mind—asks congregants to experience the mind-world barrier as porous, in a specific, limited way."[30] It takes time, practice, faith and getting used to, but those who become committed Evangelical Christians reprogram their minds, coming to believe that God listens in on their thoughts and speaks to them about life's issues large and small—interior dialogue regularly, and external statements they think they are hearing with their ears occasionally.

The anthropological insight is that in cultures or subcultures in which people expect to hear God talking to them, large numbers do. The psychological insight is that it is not even that difficult to see how a modest change in brain functioning might make that possible—and I say "modest" because the believer does not change his or her theory of mind *vis-à-vis* other people, but only where God is concerned. Nor, once we think about it, do we have too much trouble thinking of examples of similar cultural expectations and psychological adjustments outside Evangelical Christian circles. Many a mainline church body expects its ministers to hear a "call" from God before going into the ministry. From outside of the Protestant community it appears that when the would-be minister wants a call badly enough, and anxiously looks for it in his or her experience, generally it comes. And the review boards are apt to certify its legitimacy, for they share the assumption that this is not only possible but customary and sacred. I and my Jewish colleagues generally do not hear such calls, and their legitimacy might well be questioned if we did. Cultural expectations have great impact! (A nonreligious example: Freud's generation in Vienna found women inclined to hysteria, and more and more women were said to have begun exhibiting such symptoms. With the cultural expectation having faded, so has the phenomenon.)

What has this to do with the world of biblical prophets? A great deal. Clearly, from the history sketched in the previous chapter, biblical people expected to hear from God. With the conviction that God speaks through dreams and visions, lo and behold people had such dreams and visions and understood them as divine visitations. This perception may well have been enhanced by a small adaptation of their theory of mind, as Luhrmann

29. Luhrmann, *When God Talks Back*, xxii.
30. Luhrmann, *When God Talks Back*, 40.

hypothesizes for people hearing God in our time (says Ps 139:2–3, "You discern my thoughts from afar. . . . There is not a word on my tongue / But that You, O Lord, know it well"). There could be other dynamics involved as well. When people in a culture or subculture expect communication from God, they find it. They believe the evidence of their own subjective experience. Modern science and secularity raise doubts not present, or at least far less troubling, to biblical generations.

Luhrmann's interviewees heard brief messages, not whole chapters of poetry. But whether from a dream-vision or at some random moment when a voice seemed literally heard, the step from having the revelation to clothing it, as it were, in literary form, and feeling the need to preach God's urgent message repeatedly without simply saying the same words again and again, is not so difficult to imagine. Once a prophet was convinced a message was from God, I doubt the prophet felt dishonest embellishing it for dramatic impact. One of the tests Luhrmann reports her Evangelical subjects use to determine if a communication seems genuine, however, is that it fills them with peace.[31] Biblical prophets reported plenty of messages that disturbed them and were intended to distress their listeners. Nevertheless, the biblical emphasis on dreams and visions as the basis of prophecy, plus the evidence that we have seen in Jaynes and especially Luhrmann, lead me to say with some confidence that the prophets— surely most and probably all of them, perhaps even some labeled "false prophets"—were sincere. Luhrmann stresses more than once that her science cannot establish or debunk the notion that God is behind at least some of the revelations the faithful report. Neither can biblical criticism or theology.

PROPHECY AS LITERATURE AND "INSPIRATION": DUST OFF AND CHERISH THAT BIBLE!

I learned years ago that while a few contemporary Jews were shocked at the thought that God might be the order of being or some other such abstraction, plenty liked the idea. They felt liberated to hear such an idea from the pulpit. No one had told them as children (how could children have understood?) about Jewish Aristotelians or kabbalists, about Spinoza or even Mordecai Kaplan, a minority but nevertheless persistent tradition of non-personal-God thinking in Judaism. I have heard many a comment along the lines of, "You mean I don't have to suspend my natural skepticism to be a faithful Jew?!" To the contrary, since the famous story in which Jacob earned the name Israel because he had "striven with beings divine and human"

31. Luhrmann, *When God Talks Back*, 65.

(Gen 32:29), nothing could be more natural for Jews than to questions and debate everything and anything. God must not be thought of as a flesh-and-blood person, and need not be thought of as personal, person-like. Some modern Christian theologians would agree, among them Paul Tillich, who spoke of God as "the ground of being," and Charles Hartshorne, who understood God as "process." Once recognizing that God may legitimately be conceived in natural ways, a naturalistic notion of prophecy should scarcely be a surprise.

Though science has much yet to learn, we now know enough of brain operation, including the majority that goes on subconsciously, that we need not call the subconscious either demonic or divine. Most of us have had the experience of thinking about a topic or problem only to find later, when no longer consciously thinking about it, sometimes in the middle of the night, that we suddenly have a breakthrough. Our restless brains have come up with an insight or solution. The same undoubtedly happened as prophets worried about current events, the moral tenor of their times, sacrificial worship, and so on. That prophetic concerns were pondered consciously as well as unconsciously I take to be all but self-evident from the topics as well as the quality of the writing. The "writing" may often have initially been oral. Throughout history poetry in particular has been created for oral presentation, and certainly in ancient Israel as in ancient Greece and many other places sophisticated poetry came out of the minds and mouths of talented and well-practiced bards. Especially the prophecy which appears in poetry—which is the majority—could only be created by literary artists who mastered the conventions of biblical Hebrew literature.

The quality of prophetic writing is undiminished if it came from the prophets' own creative thinking, conscious and unconscious, rather than from God placing words in their mouths. The depth of prophetic insight, whether the sting of social critique or the comfort of hope proffered, is no less profound if we acknowledge it came from each prophet's own heart. They were aflame with zeal for God, giants of the spirit, endowed with exquisite religious and moral sensibilities, and at least as cognizant as we are of the sacred challenges that follow from our being active partners in, as well as beneficiaries of, the unfolding of nature and history. The culture of biblical times both shaped them and was shaped by them. They shared what they were convinced were God's concerns as well as their own. Their achievement was all the more impressive if God did not directly inspire their words. All these centuries and millennia later, their brilliance continues to shape our souls.

5

What Becomes of Revelation?

. . . And I have felt
A presence that disturbs me with the joy
Of elevated thoughts: a sense sublime
Of something far more deeply interfused,
Whose dwelling is the light of setting suns,
And the round ocean and the living air,
And the blue sky, and in the mind of man;
A motion and a spirit, that impels
All thinking things, all objects of all thought,
And rolls through all things . . .[1]

—WILLIAM WORDSWORTH

If God did not place words in prophets' mouths, or ideas in their heads, what else might give a glimpse of the divine? In the Torah Moses asks for a clear look at God, and is told that is beyond human capacity, "though I will make all My goodness pass before you" (Exod 33:19). Moses, as a mere mortal, may catch a glimpse of God as God passes by, but no more ("you

---

1. Wordsworth, "Lines Composed."

will see My back, but My face must not be seen"; 33:23). In search of traces of divinity in our world, religious people have not relied solely on verbal revelation. There are other forms of revelation, among them God in nature, God in the arts, and God in personal relationships and morality, which have inspired faith over the ages and can still give us hints of holiness, of something beyond physical being, *spirituality*, in the universe and in ourselves.

Try this little exercise. Think of the most perfect person you can imagine . . . Is physical appearance what makes her or him so perfect? Or is it her sensitivity and empathy; you feel you can trust her and develop a mutually caring relationship? Perhaps what has most impressed you is her intellectual prowess, the multiple languages she speaks, her amazing memory, quick grasp of concepts or creativity (What pictures she paints! What dances she choreographs!). While you will never find an actual person at the top of the scale in every area, no doubt you know people who excel in several, some immediately obvious to you, others—character and talents—more and more evident as you spend time together and see them enacted.

Now imagine that you have yearned to find someone displaying those traits, and you are promised by a friend that he knows just the person, and will introduce you to her. The friend pulls out a photograph and her beauty is immediately apparent. All the rest takes time to discover once you have met, but one by one this ideal person's qualities become known to you. Almost as if she were a statue with sheets thrown over her, but here it is qualities beyond the physical which mostly concern us, slowly but surely the veils fall away. What was hidden becomes revealed.

This is an elaborate metaphor for revelation. But it is God, not a person, we want revealed. So now think, analogously, of entering a deep forest, peaceful this day, though there may also be snakes or bears, and poison ivy—this is the God of everything, after all, not only of what you like. Entering the forest, at first you see only endless tree trunks and foliage. But as you go deeper there are hills and streams, animals scampering about, song birds nesting above and wildflowers. This is a place you want to be—*Ha-Makom*, "the place," one of the classic metaphors for God. As we shall see, whether the place you discover holiness is experienced like an encounter with some*one* (personal metaphor) or some*thing* (a quality such as beauty, or love—an abstract, philosophical metaphor), the more your experience grows the more that which was initially hidden becomes revealed to you.

This is revelation, the hidden or unrecognized facets of the divine becoming apparent. In neither metaphorical example does it matter if the ideal—the person or the forest—consciously intends to reveal itself. Your reaction is valid for you either way.

PURPOSE

No one can prove or disprove that such qualities of being add up to God. Belief in God or gods, however, appears to have been ubiquitous not only amongst Hebrews but universally, in ancient times. Even then, however, the "wicked man" (*rashah*) in Psalm 10 and the "fool" or "boor" (*naval*) in Psalms 14 and 53 each says to himself, "There is no God" (10:4, 14:1, 53:2). The three psalmists agree that the world is full of corrupt and foolish people, loathsome evildoers. "There is not one who does good, / not even one," says 14:3. The main issue is the lack of divine justice we discussed at some length in chapter 1: "He [God] does not call to account; / there is no God" (10:4). Then why, we might ask, even amongst the philosophically inclined, has belief in God persevered so effectively over the ages? I believe we hold on to faith because we humans are meaning-seekers, and our sense of God in the world points us to, reassures us of, meaning in life. We want to believe that there is more to life than accident, that beyond life's pleasures, intellectual and spiritual as well as physical, and despite our obvious frailty and inevitable mortality, our lives matter; they have purpose and meaning.

But we live in an empirical, scientific age. So we need some evidence that this ideal has reality behind it, and thus the conviction that life is meaningful is more than wishful thinking. We saw in chapter 2 that the notion of gods did not just suddenly pop into people's minds. As our brains evolved we found that certainly most things—and from there it is a small step to all things—did not happen without a cause. If the cause was not visible, there must have been some unseen cause. Your brain and mine infer causation too. Causes, of course, generally have causes too, the seemingly unending chain of cause and effect. When someone did not know why the rains came, or failed to, or why the neighboring tribe which never attacked before was suddenly on the march, it was easy to imagine a rain god, a goddess of war, indeed a god or goddess of almost anything important, must be involved. How nice of God or the gods to create a world, and us in it! —Or not so nice, perhaps, if your culture taught that the gods just wanted you to grow crops and raise animals to satisfy their divine hunger.[2] But generally

---

2. In the Babylonia creation myth, *Enuma Elish*, at least as old as Genesis and probably older, Marduk, king of the gods, makes a plan: "Blood I will mass and cause bones to be. / I will establish a savage, 'man' shall be his name. Verily, savage-man I will create, / He shall be charged with the service of the gods / That they might be at ease!" Pritchard, *Ancient Near East*, 36. In Deut 32:37–38, God, making fun of the gods of others, promises to take vengeance on those others. "He will say, Where are their gods, / the rock in whom they sought refuge, / Who ate the fat of their offerings / And drank their libation wine? / Let them rise up to your help. . . ," demonstrating that the gods were believed to consume the sacrifices that people brought them. (*YHWH*, on the

the point was that the world behaved as it did because the gods intended it to. Everything had a purpose, and if we wanted to prosper, we had better do what the gods wanted.

If we knew God had consciously designed each thing in the universe for a purpose, we would conclude that it is meaningful for each thing to realize its purpose. This is analogous to you or me designing a new type of screwdriver. It will be a good screwdriver if, and because, it can be used effectively to drive screws. Inferring the intent of something from its functioning is akin to reverse engineering. Human tools, of course, are consciously designed, enabling a clever engineer to examine them, perhaps take them apart, and see how they operate and thus why they were developed. The same mental process can be applied to things which were not designed by conscious designers. Planets, by the assumptions of science, came into being by the playing out of the laws of physics after the Big Bang. Likewise, human life developed by the laws of physics, chemistry and evolution. If there was no conscious designer (divine or other), however, we can still look at things that the Earth does, and that humans do, and say that, precisely like our imagined screwdriver, Earth is a good planet if it fulfills its potential well (revolving around a star, providing a home for creatures, and so on), and we can be good people if we do what we do well (passing on our genes, using our unique level of intelligence to discover how things work, loving others, etc., etc.) That is, a thought process analogous to reverse engineering may reveal that which is functionally equivalent to purpose. Purpose evident in something's function, and functionally equivalent purpose, are genuinely equivalent. We can, in a sense, find purpose built into the order of being—not human-intended purpose but, if we understand God as the order, "God-given" purpose.[3] (You might reasonably ask, can we not just as easily say that since we often do evil, as long as we do evil effectively, being really bad, we are doing what we do well, so that evil is equally our purpose? No!; for reasons to which we shall return in a moment, and again later in this chapter under "Revelation in Ethics.")

Philosopher of science Daniel Dennett reprinted a delightful cartoon in his book *Darwin's Dangerous Idea*.[4] We human beings like to think that we are at least a step if not a giant leap above the beasts and even, as the familiar psalm translation puts it, "but little lower than the angels"[5] (Ps 8:6).

---

other hand, does not eat and drink, but enjoys the "pleasing odor" (*rayach nicho'ach*) of the roasting sacrifices (Gen 8:21; Exod 29:18; Num 15:3 and 7, etc.).

3. Dennett, *Darwin's Dangerous Idea*, 212–13, or multiple passages in Dennett, *From Bacteria to Bach*, indexed under "Reverse Engineering."

4. Dennett, *Darwin's Dangerous Idea*, 330.

5. Actually more accurately translated "but little lower than gods."

The cartoonist, though, shows a primitive sea creature first climbing out of the primordial slime thinking, "Eat. Survive. Reproduce." It evolves into more reptilian-looking animals who have the same agenda: "Eat. Survive. Reproduce." And they, in turn, evolve into mammalian life, represented by a monkey also thinking its future depends on rising to the challenge: "Eat. Survive. Reproduce." Finally comes the human, who—with nature screaming the answer all around him: "Eat. Survive. Reproduce"—cannot help wondering, "What's it all about?"

Admittedly, if we are to keep our species going—not a sure bet on a warming planet, and armed with thermonuclear weapons—we had better start by worrying about survival. Eating, surviving, and reproducing are part of what life is about, though we can take them to excess (think obesity, over-population and environmental degradation). In the context of purpose and meaning we must raise the stakes beyond survival and aspire to excellence. Becoming accomplished thieves, murderers and rapists, unchecked greed and hedonism of all sorts—the evil I promised above to return to—would undermine the potential for survival. A social species, to thrive we require cooperation and thus exemplary character—trustworthiness and decency. I have met with hundreds of bereaved families and delivered eulogies for their loved ones, and survivors want their dear ones remembered for their love, for service to others, for doing their duty, for achievement—whether in businesses, art, athletics, piety or other accomplishments. Yes, if someone was a soldier, he should have been a dutiful, brave soldier, but the killing is the sad necessity, not the source of ennoblement. We humans, "reverse engineered" from what we do to what we seem designed for (whether by evolution or by a personal God), reach for excellence and meaning in life by fulfilling purposes including but beyond "Eat. Survive. Reproduce."

Different religions and philosophies of life will elaborate on such virtues differently, yet for all our differences in emphasis and vocabulary we often share similar goals, e.g., relating to God or to a realm of the sacred, striving for moral excellence, cherishing life's pleasures but transcending pure selfishness, passing our traditions on to the coming generations, doing our bit as individuals and group members to add to the store of divine intangibles—love, justice, etc. For all our disagreements (original sin?, personal immortality?, etc.) we generally agree that excellence of character for individuals, progress towards humane societies, learning and understanding, and our contributions toward a more harmonious world are what could make a life meaningful. More technically, *we sense life's meaning when we sense, exemplify or advance the order—especially the divine intangibles within that order. If the order of being plus the divine intangibles woven into it are God, experience which helps us perceive that reality is revelation.*

Since no religious person or scientist (and those are not mutually exclusive categories) would doubt that everything is part of the "ordered" universe, why not simply say that God is the universe and all that is in it? Actually, most mystics and all pantheists say precisely that. The universe, all being, is God. We could and should, in that case, regard everything as holy. But I think that blurs a classic distinction that is worth maintaining. In Hebrew the root of the word for holiness is *k-d-sh* (*kof, dalet, shin*), as in *kadosh* or *kedushah*, and it refers to something set aside, holy or sacred—or, as a verb, the setting of something aside for God-related, religious use. So if everything is holy, everything God, then, ironically, nothing is holy. The whole of being cannot be set aside from itself. I seek holiness evident within reality ("immanent" is the theological term) but not itself physical, else it would simply be more of the physical universe, not something special, "set aside." Science today insists there cannot be anything outside of the universe because space is relative to the things within it. (If there are multiple universes, as multiverse theory advocates speculate these days, there would still be nothing outside the universe of universes, so conceptually nothing has changed.[6]) Organization is neither energy nor matter, though both exhibit organization. So we may cogently understand that the universe is physical; and God is evident in the physical, indeed is the laws by which the physical operates, but not itself physical. The order of being, of course, is also the order of our being, and the way we think of the world and judge our own lives, our place in the flow of existence, strikes us, often deeply, on an emotional as well as on a rational level—"with all your heart, with all your soul, and with all your might" (Deut 6:5). This should become clearer as we look at nature, the arts and morality as revelation.

Granting that neither religion nor science, neither of which claims to fully understand ultimate truth, can prove or disprove "beyond the shadow of a doubt" that God is real and life has meaning, what in our experience points in that direction? Might there be hints somewhere that life and the world or universe have some direction, a *telos* or messianic goal, inherent in them? The order itself, subject of much of both science and religion, is such a hint. The human quest for knowledge pulls back the sheet to "reveal" God. And other aspects of our experience thrill us, "take our breath away," make everything in life suddenly seem marvelous and worthwhile. Several examples of such revelatory experience follow.

---

6. Newbauer, *Evolution and the Emergent Self*, 268.

REVELATION IN NATURE

Praise the Lord, O you who are on earth,
all sea monsters and ocean depths,
fire and hail, snow and smoke,
storm wind that executes His command,
all mountains and hills,
all fruit trees and cedars,
all wild and tamed beasts,
creeping things and winged birds,
all kings and peoples of the earth,
all princes of the earth and its judges,
youths and maiden alike,
old and young together.

(Ps 148:7–12)

At one point or another everyone has been moved, even awed, by the grandeur of sunsets or constellations, mountains or oceans, the power of hurricanes or earthquakes, the spectacle of waterfalls and—small scale too!—waves quietly lapping at the shoreline, rose blossoms, crystals. The psalmist began with heavenly phenomena—sun, moon, stars and more—all the heavenly host. Then, in the passage just above, he broadened the focus to take in more earthly sights.

Such phenomena are no less wondrous if they emerged out of the physical development, and then the evolutionary processes, from Big Bang to intelligent life. The personal God/artist/orderer whom theists hypothesize is *behind* it all is no more or less awesome than the non-personal God which *is* that order, and is thus implicit, immanent, in nature. We humans, by and large, are not its creators. Yet how blessed we feel to be part of such a creation, and to have even an inkling—and in recent times, thanks to science, deeper understanding—of how it works. Furthermore, in the era of microscopes and telescopes we have come to realize how much more there is at every level of creation than the psalmist realized, which only adds to our sense that we ourselves are small and ephemeral, and the universe, in both space and time, vast beyond our imagining, perhaps infinite ("perhaps" because we cannot, at least so far, see beyond that Big Bang, nor do we know how, or if, it will all end).

A friend who loves to ski tells me he feels closest to God at the top of mountains. And when I ask adult discussion groups when they have sensed

God or holiness in their lives, someone always says, "in the delivery room when my child was born." For all our modern sophistication, we are no less in awe of natural phenomena than psalmists and countless other sensitive souls in every culture down through the ages. The order itself, of which we are a part, thrills us. We need not fall into the perceptual bias error of seeing consciousness behind the natural world or universe to recognize the grandeur. Amazingly, yet, when you think about it, self-evidently, there is consciousness within the world and the universe—ours, at the least, and probably others'. Biologists such as Frans de Waal regard various animals as sharing consciousness, though at a simpler level than us. He reports on ape society politics, pet mammals who both crave and give affection, empathetic birds and even alligators with maternal feelings.[7] Such animal feelings may or may not be less complex than ours, but they demonstrate some degree of self-awareness as well as awareness of the needs and feelings of others. At the cosmic level, though the distances involved have at least thus far precluded our discovering the intelligent life in other worlds that many astrophysicists argue must be out there amongst the billions of stars, many of them with planets around them which might support life, there may well be more races of intelligent creatures. Thinking of these heavens, Psalms 19 and 148 echo one another in their conviction that "the heavens declare the glory of God" (19:2). What exactly in nature implies (poetically "declares") this glory? Its intricacy. Its scale. Its beauty. In a word, its order.

A fascinating book by a winner of the Nobel Prize in Physics, Dr. Frank Wilczek of the MIT Center for Theoretical Physics, may well serve as a bridge between revelation in nature and revelation in the arts and ethics. In *A Beautiful Question: Finding Nature's Deep Design*, Wilczek argues that the physical structure of the world "embod(ies) beautiful ideas."[8] The mathematical equations describing matter, which students of physics may know as "the Standard Model" or (Wilczek's preferred title) "the Core Theory," display beauty, in particular symmetry, defined as "a love of harmony, balance, and proportion."[9] He makes such observations as the following: "The equations for atoms and light are, almost literally, the same equations that govern musical instruments and sound. A handful of elegant designs support Nature's exuberant constructions."[10] Furthermore, in a final meditation on Neils Bohr's quantum physics idea of complementarity ("No one

---

7. Waal, *Bonobo and the Atheist*, 3–7.

8. Wilczek, *Beautiful Question*, 1.

9. Wilczke, *Beautiful Question*, 11.

10. Wilczek, *Beautiful Question*, 8.

perspective exhausts reality, and different perspectives may be valuable, yet mutually exclusive"[11]), Wilczek brings in a touch of morality:

Determined and Free

- I am, and you are, a material object, subject to the law of physics.
- I am, and you are, capable of making choices. I am, and you are, responsible for them.[12]

And also:

Beautiful and Not Beautiful

- The physical world embodies beauty.
- The physical world is home to squalor, suffering and strife.

In neither aspect should we forget the other.[13]

I would be a poor guide to the mathematics and physics of all this. But I am convinced that I from a theological perspective and Wilczek from a scientific perspective are working to describe the same order and finding significance, meaning, in nature, not (as some scientists have claimed) pure randomness and accident.

In sum, there is Order, and also consciousness, self-reflection, in the universe. There is intelligence. These point to, if they do not quite prove, purpose and progress—or at least they do if we accept our intuition that intelligence and understanding are infinitely desirable. Consciousness is all the more wondrous for having grown out of what began as insentient being.

REVELATION IN SCRIPTURE

They asked Ezra the scribe to bring the scroll of the Teaching of Moses with which the Lord had charged Israel. . . . Ezra opened the scroll in the sight of all the people, for he was above all the people; as he opened it all the people stood up. Ezra blessed the Lord, the great God, and all the people answered, "Amen, Amen," with hands upraised. . . . They read from the scroll of the Teaching of God, translating it and giving the sense; so they understood the reading. [And the leaders explained,] "This day is holy to the Lord your God:

11. Wilczek, *Beautiful Question*, 324.
12. Wilczek, *Beautiful Question*, 327.
13. Wilczek, *Beautiful Question*, 328.

you must not mourn or weep," for all the people were weeping as they listened to the words of the Teaching.

—NEHEMIAH 8:1B, 5–6, 8–9

We have moved from prophecy, a human phenomenon, to the immense canvas of the universe. As we turn to varieties of revelation narrower than the whole natural order, we should not leave scriptural revelation behind too quickly. Generations of insightful souls, after all, provided us with imagery and vocabulary with which to express our convictions. Though many of us do not believe that, for all their good intentions, biblical authors were literally speaking God's words, they often communicated profound messages based on their faith. Freed of the biblical literalism which belief in divine authorship suggests to fundamentalists, we can ignore misunderstandings: the world was not created in six days, for instance, or even necessarily in six periods of some measure other than twenty-four hours (Gen 1); and pi is not exactly three times the circumference of a circle (1 Kgs 7:23). We can bluntly reject, moreover, what in our time seems morally scandalous: when God is presented as commanding the genocide of Canaanites (Deut 7:1–2, 13:13–19, 20:16–18; Josh 10:39–40, 11:11–15; 1 Sam 15:3), we can condemn that as an appalling ethic unworthy of any civilization. Rather than every quarrel with Scripture shaking our faith, we can be reassured to learn that there has been some progress in several millennia.

But how do we know which biblical ideas to believe and which to regard as primitive, which commandments to feel obligated to obey and which to ignore or even condemn? We have to apply our values and convictions, knowing that they have been shaped in significant measure by our biblical heritage, but that since biblical literature grew out of a human culture (or cultures, actually) over one thousand years or so of literary productivity, Hebrew thinking displays inconsistencies and development. Which is the authentic tradition, for example: Ezra ordering exiles returned from Babylon to divorce their foreign wives (Ezra 10), or the story of Ruth, a Moabite portrayed as so loyal, selfless and noble as to be a worthy ancestor of King David (Ruth 4:13–17)? Similarly, which is the "inerrant" text and law: the Ten Commandments proclaiming that God inflicts "the guilt of the parents upon the children, upon the third and upon the fourth generations of those who reject Me" (Exod 20:5 and Deut 5:9), or the prophet Ezekiel detailing at length that individuals will only be held responsible for their own sins?(Ezek 18:1–32)? Hebrew thinking evolved over the generations, sometimes original and other times showing the influence of Canaanite, Mesopotamian and Egyptian literature, and later Persian and Hellenistic influence too. It is all there for moderns to mine for meanings, much of it—but frankly not all—great literature, provocative, profound and endlessly fascinating.

The rabbinic Jewish tradition has found the process of studying, interpreting and even arguing vociferously over Torah (not just the five books of Moses, but the whole literary tradition which includes and grows from roots in the Bible) to be intrinsically fascinating and meaningful. When I hear fundamentalists arguing that as soon as you say something in the Bible is false or morally objectionable you have destroyed the credibility of Scripture, for you can no longer count on God's word, I find such faith impressive, but simplistic. No text, ancient or modern, interprets itself. We bring our world of ideas to the ancient texts, as did their authors, and must decide what to take from them. There is an ongoing dialogue not only between moderns and ancients, but between generations of serious interpreters in between. The author of Genesis 22, to cite an obvious example, strikes most of us as holding up Abraham as a model of faith for his willingness to sacrifice his son to God. But some rabbinic (thus postbiblical) interpreters were as shocked in pondering this as we are, and so insisted Abraham misunderstood.[14] With such dramatically different interpretations offered to serious students by classic sources, we not only may, but must decide for ourselves what to take away from the reading, and may add our own insights. As I like to put it, Jews are called to take Scripture seriously but not always literally. In our day, to throw in two urgent contemporary examples, many of us cannot accept as models the implicit low status of women in the Bible and the condemnation of male homosexuality (Lev 18:22). "Love your neighbor as yourself," rather, should apply to all neighbors (Lev 19:18). Modern biblical studies can help us to come closer to what the biblical generations understood in Scripture, but postbiblical interpretations are also part of our heritage and worthy of taking seriously.

The germane question as we read Scripture—commandments as well as narratives and other biblical writings—is whether they direct human thought to God and give us guidance for living our lives. When I was in rabbinical school a renowned rabbi and scholar who had recently produced an outstanding Torah commentary for our Reform Jewish movement, W. Gunther Plaut, came to campus to talk to students. In one of the sessions he spoke, not surprisingly, of the profound wisdom of Torah. Full of chutzpah, I asked, "But Dr. Plaut, do you believe that God actually wrote Torah?" He answered, "I don't know if God wrote it. What I know is that when I study Torah and rabbinic literature, I sense the living presence of God." He may

---

14. *Midr. Rab., Gen. Rab.* 56:8. (God speaks to Abraham:) "Did I tell thee, slaughter him? No! But 'Take him up.' Thou hast taken him up. Now bring him down."

(or may not, but he was certainly well aware of twentieth-century Jewish philosophy) have consciously echoed Franz Rosenzweig and Martin Buber, existentialist thinkers and biblical scholars who knew they sometimes felt addressed by God when reading Torah, but also found some biblical passages beyond belief. Where the great revelation story of Sinai was concerned, they agreed that God reveals God's presence—based on which Moses, who thought in human categories, wrote down the Decalogue.[15] When individuals who take their religious traditions seriously want to sense God's presence (a subjective feeling, unverifiable by anyone else), we customarily immerse ourselves in Scripture, a time-tested "place" to which we have gone for that purpose for well over two thousand years.

But cannot a Christian, then, or a Muslim claim that in the same way they encounter God in their Scriptures? For that matter, cannot Hindus, Buddhists and others make the same claim? Of course they can. Why would we not expect the universal God to be universally available for all to encounter? Imagine how much richer, both intellectually and spiritually, we would all be if, having first learned the basics of our own holy books and ideas, we also studied one another's. Not that we would all agree, even inside and especially outside the "family" of Western religions. But we would gain a deeper appreciation of the manifold ways to understand God and the human condition. "How many are Your works, O Lord, / with wisdom have you made them all; / the earth is full of Your creations" (Ps 104:24). Scriptures are revelatory without each having to be understood as the sole and perfect truth. Moreover, literary and other artistic expressions with only indirect, if that, reference to religion may also come to be recognized as revelatory, for religion is about the whole of life, not only about a narrow "religious" realm.

REVELATION IN LITERATURE AND THE ARTS

I like to think of the Wordsworth epigraph at the beginning of this chapter as part of my personal "spiritual landscape," but so are many non-religious poetic passages which move me. Great literature gives us an emotional feel as well as a cognitive portrait of experience. Others, obviously, may find the meaning of life clearer in, or their own thoughts more elevated by, different poems, plays and novels—the best expressions of the individuals and

15. On Rosenzweig, see Borowitz, *Laymen's Introduction*, 80: "Unlike traditional Judaism, Rosenzweig does not believe God reveals words, statements, utterances. All God gives in revelation is himself, his presence." For Buber, see Buber, *I and Thou*, 110: "Man receives, and he receives not a specific 'content,' but 'a Presence, a Presence as power.'"

cultures that shaped them. Art can help us see, feel and understand differently. I have focused on Scripture and literary art because these can make logical points even as they also appeal to emotion. But all of the arts exist at the intersection of thought and emotion. Without what can sometimes be the distraction of words and elaborated ideas, other arts can often be more effective in expressing emotion, a key component of spirituality (which we will explore further in the next chapter). We turn, then, briefly to the arts more broadly: music, painting, sculpture, architecture, dance—you name it!

Art—like everything else, but shaped intentionally for the purpose—is an expression of the order of being as artist, work of art, performers (if any) and audience interact. When we more than simply reflect, but refine this expression, trying to capture the essence of experience, we help ourselves catch views of the (not-so-hidden) order. Everything owes its existence to God-as-order: psalms and garbage, supernovae and mosquitos, you and me—everything. But much of what we encounter in daily life, at least until we meditate on it and sometimes even then, does not turn our hearts or minds to the realm of meaning. That is the challenge of art.

Music, and particularly music without words, may illustrate the point. A composer, whether of brief melodies, symphonies or jazz, employs instruments (and sometimes voices) to arrange sound so as to evoke reaction in the listener(s), usually a reaction of pleasure. Hearing evolved at least in part to enable communication. Think of the shrieks of apes and other animals warning that a predator has been sighted in the area. What the mechanism in our ears is actually sensitive to is simply vibration in the air, which is translated into neural signals interpreted in the brain as sounds coming from closer or farther away, from one direction or another, higher or lower, harsher (banging, shrieking, etc.) or milder (wind stirring leaves, the hum of bees, and so on). Furthermore, the human vocal apparatus enables us to make sounds which may be combined into words and languages to communicate more and more abstract concepts, but also to sing. There are a wealth of musical instruments with widely differing sorts of sounds (the same note sounds different on strings, horns or woodwinds). What we experience as sound, in other words, is just vibration, but the brain turns it into something capable of communicating an infinite variety of moods and messages. There is no agreement about whether music (reverse engineered, as discussed above) was intended for more than basic communication. Clearly we take pleasure in some sounds or harmonious combinations of sounds, and some more than others. In Darwinian terms, that is, music may be an accidental byproduct of communication, or may have broader function making it adaptive in itself—singing a child to sleep, seducing a potential mate, dancing rhythmically to strengthen communal solidarity or perhaps please the gods. By now much music is purely about aesthetic pleasure.[16]

In any event, descriptions of how music works stress that the ordered arrangement of varying notes, tunes and harmonies creates expectation, and pleasure in the fulfillment of the expectation, or surprise when the composer or musician varies the melody and frustrates such expectation, not to mention the potential to go faster or slower, or to make the listener wait a moment for the expected denouement. All this and more (handing the melody over to different instruments or voices for repetition or variation, etc., etc.), creates—by culturally established rules—varying degrees of pleasure. The communication here is generally more of emotion than ideas, or some of each, especially if the music includes words. In the creation of mood, dissonance as well as harmony may be experienced as beautiful—a fact we know from the acceptance of dissonance into modern music, and from cross-cultural studies which have found admittedly rare, but still significant, examples of discord as the musical norm.[17]

The magic of music is all about variations on order, and every culture develops them. The variations on physical order and cultural expectation, and the ever-evolving "rules" of what is considered aesthetically pleasing, are infinite. Our brains try to make sense of the world by discerning pattern, order and its implications. Where music is concerned, at some point pleasant crosses the line to beautiful, and thence even to exciting or exquisite. If—our premise all along—God is not the creator of order, but the order itself, God is lurking in music, or at least in what people find to be the best music.

We could go on in similar fashion with each branch of the arts. Where simple communication ends, art begins. At some point aesthetics becomes more the goal than any message or pragmatic function. Order—divine—and response—human—merge. The order, both the formative/organizational order and the divine intangibles—beauty, truth—evoke our conviction that there is more to our lives than we most often take note of. In the hands of skilled artists the order (based reciprocally in the world and in our perceptions) captures attention, enthusiasm, even rapture. Ergo: revelation.

As some feel closest to God in nature, others feel transcendence hearing music and—the eye having evolved to interpret light as did the ear to interpret vibration—some are touched most deeply at an art museum, a temple, the ballet, and so on and so forth. We shall not take time to go through every form of art. But the interaction of perception, rational analysis and

16. Levitan, *This Is Your Brain on Music*, 241–61.
17. Brandt and Eagleman, *Runaway Species*, 126–27.

emotional reaction lead to "inspiration," our sense of transcendence and meaning. The order of nature, the conventions of culture, for some of the arts the thoughtful sensitivity of performers, and ideally openness to the experience on the part of audiences are, on those blessed occasions when they come together powerfully, revelatory. The local classical music radio station in the Dallas–Fort Worth metroplex has been running a series of advertisements each of which begins, "Imagine a world without this . . . ," after which they play a few bars of Bach's "Jesu Joy of Man's Desiring," Debussy's "Claire de Lune," Beethoven's "Pastorale Symphony," or other icons of musical taste. A rock, jazz or pop station could do the same, of course, as could a television station with the visual arts. Though we differ in our tastes, the enthusiasm of "You just know there's a God when you experience that" is not an overstatement.

Are there truly atheists, or only people who do not want to apply the word "God" to that which moves them and helps give meaning to their lives?

REVELATION IN ETHICS

We must somehow take a wider view, look at the whole landscape, really see it, and describe what's going on here. Then we can at least wail the right question into the swaddling band of darkness, or, if it comes to that, choir the proper praise.[18]

—ANNIE DILLARD

Imagine if there were evidence of moral values in the world even apart from human societies. Would that not suggest a benevolence to the order, whether or not there is a conscious creator God? In recent years science has been finding more and more such evidence. In order to consider the goodness we find revelatory, we will also, of course, need to deal with what we regard as evil.

When something promotes our thriving or satisfaction in the world, we call it good, and when something undermines our well-being, especially if it causes us to suffer, we call it bad or even—for intensely bad phenomena—evil. In religious terms we sometimes label such good and evil blessings and curses, logically tying them to our idea of God and thus our sense of meaning. When we learn more, or think more deeply, we may realize that what we thought bad was good, or vice versa, as when pain is the body's signal of a serious danger ("Every cloud has a silver lining") or career success brings heavy

18. Dillard, *Pilgrim at Tinker Creek*, 11.

and time-consuming responsibilities and worries ("Be careful what you wish for; you may get it"). Normal human desires are neither good nor evil until we take action. Acted out as greed, lust, assault or unfair competition, selfish drives may get us into trouble. But the classic rabbis were correct asserting that without such drives "no one would build a house, marry, beget children . . . or engage in business" (*Midr. Rab., Gen. Rab.* 9:7). *The basic drives are only bad when acted out in extreme or illicit manner, "doing what comes naturally" only bad when we hurt ourselves, others or the ecosystem which sustains us all.*

Death too is a natural part of life, which has an end as well as a beginning. By the laws of physics, which is to say as part of the divine order of being, everything biological eventually degrades. To maintain energy, and for bodies to grow and repair themselves, we need food, and every other living thing needs nutrition of some sort as well. The food chain, with nature renewing itself in endless cycles, is a necessary—and actually quite clever from a design perspective—aspect of nature. Most of us love to eat! It is nice being at the top of the food chain, though we too will ultimately decay and contribute ourselves back to the cycle. Even with adequate nutrition our physical systems will wear out eventually. In the grand system, the inevitability of death is part of the maintenance of life. This is not evil, as if everything existed for our sake and we are entitled to thrive forever. We cannot even declare all violence as inherently evil, as the food chain requires it (you and I could, at least in theory, become vegetarians; eagles and crocodiles, and countless other creatures, could not). If we were designing the system ourselves, we could scarcely do better than to provide food for all (a classic Jewish blessing is "Blessed are You, O God, Who provides food for all"). We enjoy countless aspects of the ecological system, for we evolved to take advantage of it. On balance, most of us regard life as good and understand that death, like birth, is the price of our participation. Death does not sap the natural system of goodness and meaning. What is genuinely evil, however, is humans torturing or murdering one another, hatred, aggressive war, oppression, and so on—freely chosen and therefore morally fraught behaviors.

We experience natural disasters, the "acts of God" we spoke of in the first chapter, as evil. In fact, however, while they are evidence against a conscious God running the world for our benefit, the drifting of tectonic plates or occasional extreme wind, rain and lightning are simply the way things are—morally neutral on the grand scale, like death. Such events are simply the way things work in a world we most often find hospitable and have little desire to leave.

But is there any evidence that good values, moral principles, are a natural part of the system? Can we, that is, argue that the order is more benign than not? In the evolution of life we see a movement from simplicity to complexity, the latter making possible intelligence, consciousness and then morality, all of which we certainly regard as advances—which implies purpose. My goal in what follows is to demonstrate that, in the process, certain meta-moral principles are built into the structure of being, especially the subset of being consisting of living creatures. While neither personally nor as a species is the whole natural system "about us," the system is good and we savor our part.

Rocks, molecules, atoms and energy in its various forms simply do what the order of nature has "programmed" them to do. And God does not have to create the program if, as I have argued, God *is* the program. Once life originates, moreover, certain behaviors turn out to work better than others. This is only proto-morality, we might say, but the ethical ball, as it were, begins growing like a snowball rolling downhill, emerging as full morality when conscious choice enters the equation. (Genesis, we note in passing, does not introduce moral quandaries in the first chapter, creation, either.) Moral issues appear when the first person has to deal with a second one and then with a growing family, the Eden myth of chapters 2–4. Then Genesis begins to display ancient Hebrew attitudes about obedience and disobedience (Adam and Eve), integrity and lack thereof (the snake), patience, family loyalty, murder (Cain and Abel), and so on. Human understanding of the concepts of obedience, truthfulness and not murdering are not commanded, but simply assumed. That is a problem if morality requires divine commandments. In our day, however, we recognize some values evolved even before there were people. They are our inheritance from the evolutionary process.

Science tells us that the first living things, bacteria, appeared nearly four billion years ago. They were and are one-celled organisms, lacking even a nucleus, much less a brain. But they learned by trial and error that it was wise to stay close to nutrients. This "decision" had to be—and remains—strictly chemical, not mental. The wonder, furthermore, does not stop there. When nutrients are not readily available, bacteria band together in groups and sense how many other bacteria are with them. They line up to defend a territory—or not!—depending on their numbers and thus their group strength. Furthermore, writes neuroscientist Antonio Damasio of the University of Southern California:

> . . . they even assume what can only be called a sort of "moral attitude." The closest members of their social group, their family so to speak, are mutually identifiable by the surface molecules they produce or chemicals they secrete, which are in turn related

to their individual genomes. But groups of bacteria have to cope
with the adversity of their environments and often have to compete with other groups in order to gain territory and resources.
For a group to be successful, its members need to cooperate.

Furthermore, these one-celled and non-brained organisms keep track
of who helps and who does not, later not cooperating with—freezing out, as
it were—those who did not help.[19] That is fair. In Darwinian fashion, then,
cooperators survive and reproduce better than non-cooperators. Bacteria,
needless to say, know nothing of altruism or punishment, of morality in the
abstract. That awareness awaits billions of years of evolution when brains,
and then language, evolve. Nevertheless, here at the beginning of life we
already have rudimentary cooperation as a behavior naturally superior to
non-cooperation. We also get a first glimpse of justice as a social value.

Another variety of one-celled organism, archaea, have much in common with bacteria, and biologists label the two of them "prokaryotes." At
some point, it is confidently theorized, a bacterium and an archaeon, with
somewhat different abilities due to their separate evolution, bumped into
one another. On at least one occasion, instead of bouncing off each other or
one eating the other, one "engulfed" the other and "found itself fitter—more
competent in ways that mattered—than it had been as an unencumbered
soloist." Suddenly it was a two-celled organism, destined, moreover, to reproduce and maintain the talents of both by cell division (and later by other
evolved forms of reproduction, including sexual). Each multicelled organism that survived did so because it could do something (or multiple things)
better when its cells cooperated. Competition and even aggression remain
very much with us throughout evolutionary history, up to and including us
humans—and not only for food, but for whatever a given organism or species needs or wants. Yet when prokaryotes, and later more complex species,
stumbled on the tactic of cooperation, each of them, and each colony of
them, improved its odds of survival.[20]

Specialized cells would evolve—blood cells, skin cells, brain cells, etc.,
etc.—making possible complex animals, and ultimately the most complex,
humans. Furthermore, within each of our bodies is a huge population of
microorganisms, our "microbiota," including bacteria, archaea, fungi and
viruses, without which we could not live. Digestion of food in our gut, for
example, requires them. They are not really "us" (where digestion is concerned, antibiotics may kill off many, but the survivors—or foods rich in
them, such as yogurt—can help repopulate them). Our subjective sense of

19. Damasio, *Strange Order of Things*, 19–20.
20. Dennett, *From Bacteria to Bach*, 7–8.

being a single entity is valid for our single consciousness attached to a body (the "me," the "ego," the intelligent self reading this book), but the symbionts without which we would die could lead us to say without exaggeration that each of us is a team. Again, note cooperation on a huge scale built into the structure of life.

Mothers in some species leave newly hatched or born offspring on their own, producing enough of them that even if some, or most, are eaten by predators or fall victim to the elements, enough survive to continue the species. As animals over the eons of evolution grew more complex, however, many later-evolving animal mothers developed an emotional bond to their (generally fewer) children, and fed and protected them—cared for them (note the emotional overtone; we humans might say "loved" them)—which could well be the genesis of love as an emotional basis for a pragmatic commitment. Should we dismiss such maternal devotion as mere self-interest, suggesting these mothers are only concerned about passing on their genes? No! We can imagine that at some time in the distant evolutionary past some mothers displayed caring and others did not. Neither had the vaguest inkling of what caring, love or genetics are about. But if goodness, as we suggested above, is about what leads us to thrive, it is plain why the caring mothers produced more surviving offspring than the uncaring ones. There is a moral distinction between them. And once maternal love evolved (and there are traits that evolve separately in more than one species simply because they work so well), it was there, encoded in the genes, not only for the children and grandchildren, but for further species descending from the early caring species. Similarly, if animal mothers develop such a trait, passing it on to their offspring, might we not expect to find that some of their male offspring would get it too? Of course. And without denying that nature is particularly influenced by the pragmatic need to pass along genes, which explains why it is adaptive for parent animals, or its close relatives in a pack or school, for that matter, to risk their lives defending their young, we also hear of all sorts of animals who display affection for and even "adopt"—providing a nest, food and protection—animals of another species. This is not universal by any means. A guide showing my wife and me a beach and nesting ground for sea lions in southern Australia explained how mother sea lions go to sea hunting fish, some of which they bring back to feed their pups. Sometimes the mother never returns, most likely having fallen victim to great white sharks. The orphaned pups whine pathetically but are left to die by mothers focused only on feeding their own offspring. On the other hand, biologist and primatologist Frans de Waal provides multiple examples of chimpanzees adopting orphaned baby chimps.[21] We also know stories of abandoned birds adopted by mother birds of other species, and dolphins rescuing drowning sailors by bringing them to shore. An evolutionary biologist who heard me give a talk on some of this material responded, "Yes, but how many dolphins may have taken the drowning man further out to sea?" A reasonable point, I admit, but it does not refute de Waal's larger thrust:

> Both human and animal altruism may be genuine . . . in that it lacks ulterior motives. This is true to the point that we have trouble suppressing it. James Rilling, an Emory colleague of mine, concluded from neuroimaging experiments that we have "emotional biases toward cooperation that can only be overcome with effortful cognitive control." Think about it: this means that our first impulse is to trust and assist; only secondarily do we weigh the option of not doing so, for which we need sound reasons. . . . Rilling further showed that when normal people aid others, brain areas associated with reward are activated. Doing good feels good.[22]

Thus to cooperation and justice add compassion, love and altruism. We could go on with empathy and sympathy, reciprocal altruism (otherwise known as "the Golden Rule"), self-sacrifice and more.[23] We inherit not only powerful hungers and aggression—broadly speaking, our selfishness—but also moral impulses and sometime self-sacrificial generosity from biological as well as cultural (including religious) evolution. Much of our morality is hardwired, in our genes and brains. We are clearly not always good. Yet, that first unreflective animals, and eventually theologically and philosophically sophisticated humans, are so often good testifies to the bias towards goodness over evil built into the structure of being. Ethics and morality are, in a word, revelatory.

❖ ❖ ❖

We have seen, then, that even without verbal revelation we may find intimations of divinity, revelation, and in the process satisfy some of our yearnings for purpose, meaning and self-transcendence:

- *What an awesome universe we are part of (revelation in nature)!*

---

21. Waal, *Bonobo and the Atheist*, 44–47.

22. Waal, *Bonobo and the Atheist*, 48–49.

23. For more explanation of these, see section on "Evolved Values" in Mecklenburger, *Our Religious Brains*, 123–28. Also see Wilson, *Meaning of Human Existence*, chapter 6, especially p. 63.

- *How beautiful and profound are our works as well as God's (revelation in Scripture and in the arts)!*

- *How humbling and challenging to think that we can be, each and all, better people making a better world (revelation in morality)!*

Faith, then, has its place, taking us a bit beyond, without contradicting, what we can establish empirically.

We turn next to a reassessment of religious activities that have nurtured and guided us over the centuries: faith, prayer and ritual, and religious institutions such as synagogues and churches.

6

Filling the Pews Again

Faith, Spirituality, and Worship

I rejoiced when they said to me,
"We are going to the House of the Lord."

—Ps 122:1

A few summers ago my wife and I found ourselves on the Jersey Shore with children and grandchildren. On the beach our four-year-old grandson, who loved the nice, calm swimming pool at home, was keeping his distance from the ocean. If you are not very tall, ocean waves are scary. After he had watched everyone else go in and out of the water a couple of times, I urged him to come on in with me, assuring him that I would not let go of his hand. We slowly waded out into the water, waves breaking against us. Frightened of the water, but trusting of me, Will looked up and said, "Grandpa, are you sure this is a good idea?"

That memory came back to me some time later on a stormy night at DFW Airport. We sat for forty-five minutes on the tarmac waiting for the hold on all flights to be lifted. Finally we were cleared and took off. We were fine for a few minutes as the plane climbed. I saw lightning flash. Then suddenly the ride got a lot rougher. The plane bumped up and down, and then dropped so violently that the magazine in the seat pocket in front of me flew out. My stomach seemed to go up as my body, thanks to the seat belt, stayed down. Several people screamed. "God, get us safely through this!" I thought, and had no doubt that mine was not the only prayer being said. The turbulence continued for a couple of minutes and a quotation popped into my mind. "Grandpa, are you sure this is a good idea?" Was a cosmic Father hanging on to us? Is God always there to keep us safe and secure?

FAITH AND BLESSINGS

The Hebrew word for faith is *emunah*—same root meaning as *amen*, which of course we say at the end of many a prayer to indicate that we give our assent to what has just been said. Someone says something like, "Praised are You, O God . . . who brings forth bread from the earth," and we say "Amen," meaning, "I gratefully share the understanding that the food is a blessing that I did not create." The farmer, to be sure, facilitated the process, as did the baker. The blessing is over bread, not grain. Still, the farmer can only provide grain for bread if he or she has seed, and even then will fail if there is no rain— which we do not create either. In any number of situations Jews and others praise God for the world in which we, with help from forces beyond us, can survive and even prosper. Whether the words are classic blessing formulas from the prayer book or products of our own more spontaneous spirituality, we end on "Amen." We do know about droughts, locust plagues, tomato beetles, and all sorts of things which can, with this as with other blessings, go wrong. Starvation remains a real threat to many in the world even today. Chances are, however, that we will be fine; there will be groceries in the store when we go to buy them, and we will be grateful. Amen. We believe. Where food is concerned, in our era that is a reasonable belief.

Consider blessings not about physical things such as food, but about more abstract matters. Each time we say wedding blessings—seven of them, for example, at a Jewish wedding—we are saying that we more than just hope (they have courted!; they each know they are taking a momentous step), but less than know for sure (we have a 50 percent divorce rate in our society!) that this match will go well—our fervent prayer and desire for them. We sense that the whole history and structure of our lives and society—people growing up and falling in love, and making more babies to continue the cycle—all of that and more is worthy of our affirmation. So we say amen, tying the moment to our religious tradition. Love is one of those divine intangibles, after all. So we affirm, believe, have faith, that the couple, and to some extent we who share their moment of joy, have been blessed. Many couples will fail. Enough will succeed that the system—human nature, societal norms, the flow of generations—is worth acknowledging as sacred. So we acknowledge a holy moment (*kadosh*, set aside for sacred purpose, relating us to God) and say, in effect, may this marriage go well! Amen and amen—seven times over!

Faith is our confidence that life, by the nature of the world and its God, can be lived meaningfully, despite the undeniable risks. In this sense, I suspect, everyone has faith, agnostics and atheists included. My four-year-old grandson had faith in me as we waded into the waves. The evidence was that I was a pretty reliable guy, old enough and big enough to keep my head, and his!, above water. On the airplane I had faith that the radar and wind-velocity gauges, and the weather team first holding and then releasing our plane to fly, as well as the presumably experienced pilot, were all reliable. I said a little prayer, anyway. It couldn't hurt, right? I do understand that what really kept the plane up was its aerodynamic design, and all that talent both on the ground and in the cockpit. Why say the prayer, though, if I do not believe that order hears prayers, but rather just continues to operate? In retrospect, an emotional surge motivated me. I could legitimately say I was reminding myself that the order was consistent and thus could be expected to keep the plane in the air, which is to say there was nothing hypocritical about a religious person offering a prayer. But I had no time for such abstractions; I was yearning for God to do something special right now. I do not believe God does miracles, violates the divine nature, which is what it would mean for God to intervene and suspend the laws of meteorology, physics or anything else as a personal favor to me or the others on the plane in response to prayer. I acknowledge my humanity and the inescapable place of emotion in religion. I can occasionally employ anthropomorphic God talk (and believers in the personal God may use philosophical God talk). No harm done; God is the same as we change metaphors.

Faith and prayer, we have just seen, reinforce beliefs and values. This includes our moral values. We pray that leaders will lead wisely, that we and people of different races, nationalities and other differences will empathize with each other and learn to treat one another with respect. We pray for the well-being and healing of the sick and suffering. We pray for peace. And here, precisely, is where yearning, hope and personal rectitude come in. Experience has taught us that harmony will not consistently be achieved. Wisdom and religious ideals teach us this will happen only if we each do our share. What we know is that things *can* be better. But it takes faith to keep plugging away through the disappointments. Faith, again, not contradicting the evidence (things really can get better) but taking us beyond the evidence (I could have had a heart attack in the water; pilot error or unexpected wind shear could have brought down the airplane). Screaming in terror or despair would have conferred no advantage in these or other such situations, but faith does: it helps you through them.

We each live by faith every day that we get up in the morning. We figure—nearly always correctly—that we will make it through the day. So from time to time, in gratitude, Jews say *Shehecheyanu*, the blessing which praises God "for keeping us alive, sustaining us and enabling us to reach this time." Other religions, indubitably, have comparable prayers of thanks. We trust God, whether as personal God, order of being, process in history, creator or redeemer—pick your own preferred image!—with our lives. We trust God with our deaths—and our griefs, which is probably harder as loved ones disappear. Constant worry and fear would be debilitating. Faith is sustaining. Faith itself is one of the blessings that enrich our lives, which for all their frailty are yet touched by love, joys, satisfactions and infinite possibilities.

RITUAL: SPIRITUALITY AND PHYSICALITY

Spirituality, by which I mean the subjective feeling of holiness, or of being in the presence of God, is not simply a warm and fuzzy feeling, but a real phenomenon, demonstrable via brain scans in the laboratory. If we understand what it is, perhaps we can help people achieve more of it. We need to consider some generalizations about the way our brains function, then also consider their implications for religious experience. Put it all together and we should have a deeper understanding of spirituality and its place in worship.

Dr. Andrew Newberg and colleagues, nearly twenty years ago, found via nuclear medicine scans that the area in the brain which keeps track of one's orientation to the environment (e.g., standing or sitting, next to or above) and of the boundary between oneself and the world becomes quiescent—nearly turned off, as it were—during Buddhist monks' meditation and Christian nuns' intense centering prayer (in which the individual nun focuses "on a particular prayer, word or passage from the Bible"). With dramatically less awareness of the orientation and boundaries of the self there is a sense of oneness with what would otherwise be thought of as beyond the self, oneness with all of being for the Buddhists, and with Christ for the Christians.[1] In other words, feelings of spirituality were evoked when meditating Buddhists and Christians lost some connection to the here and now. It is notable that the Christians, employing words, had more activity in language centers of the brain, but they still had in common with

---

1. Newberg and D'Aquili, *Why God Won't Go Away*, 1–10. Newberg and Waldman, *Why We Believe*, 172–78.

the Buddhists the feeling of mystical *union* with that-which-was-beyond-them—which we might call the *transcendent*.

Research using brain scans, especially functional magnetic resonance imaging (fMRI), has continued. A small but very interesting study recently appeared which found that both individuals who are and those who are not self-identified as religious experienced what they felt as "spirituality" when read a simple narrative. The narratives were based on what participants had previously identified as experiences which connected them to "something bigger than oneself, a oneness or strong force which may be experienced as an energy, force, higher power, G-d, deity or transcendent figure or consciousness." Dr. Lisa Miller and colleagues at Harvard and Columbia Universities found various areas of the brain were effected, including, significantly, the prime area Newberg et al. had identified (Newberg said "parietal area" and the new study says "inferior parietal lobule"). Again, the scans show the area was quieted, not stimulated, in the experience. Moreover, such spiritual experiences help individuals to relax, and to calm anxiety.[2] If instead of defining spirituality (as above) as "the subjective feeling of holiness, or of being in the presence of God," we say "a sense of deep or impactful relation with the transcendent," we now have non-religious spirituality little if any different from religious spirituality. At one time "non-religious spirituality" might have sounded like an oxymoron, but in recent years many report being "spiritual but not religious" (think 1960s Age of Aquarius and, more generally, New Age spirituality). I have argued elsewhere that we experience our spirituality through the lens, in effect, of our religion or other structure of meaning, learned by many of us as children, and all of us via cultural influence and personal experience.[3] This study of non-religious spirituality is further evidence of the universality of spirituality. One can imagine other experiences—say awe at natural or artistic beauty, or at courageous acts; or evocative ritual, similarly quieting the sense of individuality and connecting people in the process to the transcendent. In this recent study, after all, it was not only the primary experience, but also hearing the story of such experience—a common religious exercise—that evoked spirituality. Furthermore, many of the religiously faithful would attest to finding much religious literature, psalms for example, calming and even anxiety reducing. The Newberg studies were of mystics, but the Miller group study finds spirituality in a more random sample of healthy young adults.

Emotion, then, not only the dialing up or down of intellectual attention, needs to be added to this picture. For several decades Dr. Antonio

---

2. Miller et al., "Neural Correlates," 2331–2338.

3. Mecklenburger, *Our Religious Brains*, 37–59.

Damasio has been one of the leaders in the revolutionary field of neuroscience. Reading Damasio one learns that our brains are always operating on two levels, rational and emotional. Emotion is present even when we think we are being purely rational. Early in his book *Descartes' Error: Emotion, Reason, and the Human Brain*, Damasio discusses the sad plight of people who, due to serious accidents or cancer lesions, lose the use of certain areas of the brain which are largely responsible for emotion. Otherwise healthy, we might expect that they would become super-rational and efficient, like Mr. Spock in the *Star Trek* series. In laboratory tests they are, indeed, fully capable of rational analysis—categorizing things, delineating options for action. But often they are scarcely able to make a decision. Damasio writes, for instance, of giving a patient a choice between two dates, a few days apart, for his next appointment:

> The patient pulled out his appointment book and began consulting the calendar. The behavior that ensued, which was witnessed by several investigators, was remarkable. For the better part of half an hour, the patient enumerated reasons for and against each of the two dates. . . . It took enormous discipline to listen to all of this without pounding the table and telling him to stop, but we finally did tell him, quietly, that he should come on the second of the alternative dates. His response was equally calm and prompt. He simply said, "That's fine." Back went the appointment book into his pocket, and he was off.[4]

What this shows is that rarely, if ever, do we make purely rational decisions. Even for the simplest decisions we have to care, an emotional input, to decide.

Furthermore, emotions and feelings ("feelings," according to Damasio, occurring when you become aware that you have an emotion) are not strictly between your ears. "All emotions use the body as their theater," Damasio writes in his book *The Feeling of What Happens*.[5] The brain monitors changeable bodily states. You are grief-stricken, fearful, or deeply worried, and say it feels like your stomach is in knots. Or you charge into danger and people around you say you "really have guts." We do, in fact, react "viscerally"—in the gut—to stressful situations. When your brain gets the message that your gut is upset, *then* it knows *you* are upset. On the positive side (and more fun at your next cocktail party), take a pencil and put it long-ways, from corner to corner, in your mouth. Your mouth and your cheeks are now in a smile-like position; you cannot frown. Now try to think angry or

4. Damasio, *Descartes' Error*, 193–94.
5. Damasio, *Feeling of What Happens*, 51.

sad thoughts. That guy who drives you crazy is at it again! Someone you care about is gravely ill. These thoughts ought to upset you, but your brain, monitoring your body, is getting the message that you are alright. You know this is a trick you are playing on yourself, but it works anyway. Your brain did not learn to keep track of the emotions your body was signaling when you really mean them. It assumes you mean them. Body and brain trust one another, for they are parts of one whole self; the brain is an organ of the body, not a separate being.

There are lots of different emotions and different shadings and degrees of emotions, generated internally from your own thoughts or externally from your experience. But to be translated into feelings, to become conscious, there must be a physical, which is to say bodily, trigger.

Turning to theology, think of a time you have sensed holiness or "felt at one" with forces and realities way beyond yourself, a time—you might be so bold as to say—you have sensed God in your life. Perhaps you were in the delivery room and your child had just taken a first breath. Or perhaps it was Erev Yom Kippur and a fine cellist brought the soulful melody of *Kol Nidre* to life. Or you looked out over some extraordinarily awe-inspiring natural phenomenon and familiar words came naturally to mind: "The heavens declare the glory of God" (Ps 19:2), or maybe Wordsworth, "And I have felt / A presence which disturbs me with the joy / Of elevated thoughts."[6] Maybe you gasped, breathing in—inspiring! At such moments you react emotionally, triggering a physical reaction in the body that, back in your brain, brings the feeling to your grateful consciousness. "Wow! Get a load of that! Remember this moment! Hallelujah!" Then maybe your rational faculty kicks in: "I think I should say *Shehecheyanu*";[7] "get the camera"; "Dear God: I love it when this happens and I know you are out there"; or perhaps even, ". . . suddenly life makes sense and has meaning, though I lack the words to capture it adequately." The words can come later, if at all, for the primary experience is a largely emotional reaction: spirituality! Spirituality is not purely emotional; it is rational *also*. Your particular variety of spirituality will hang on the framework of your understanding of life, your structure of meaning. For me that will be a significantly Jewish structure of meaning, though it is harmless if Wordsworth sneaks in, or Beethoven. For others the spiritual response may include whatever else is part of *their* intellectual or spiritual landscape. *Spirituality has cognitive content, also, but is first and foremost emotional.*[8]

---

6. Wordsworth, "Tintern Abbey," 78–79.

7. Classic Jewish blessing recited upon reaching a special moment.

8. Mecklenburger, *Our Religious Brains*, 50–59.

What has that to do with how our worship works? If Damasio is correct that "all emotions use the body as their theater" (not some emotions, not most; "all"); and if Newberg is on target declaring religious experience a real phenomenon, a testable, documentable change in the brain; and if I, pondering the science, am right that emotion is at the heart of the experience of spirituality, then we dare not let people sit quietly in our sanctuaries, presumably relating intellectually to the service content, but rarely doing much more than rising for a special prayer. —Not that, for example, Jews reciting *Va'anachnu*, rising to "bow the head and bend the knee" before the *Melech Malchei Hamlachim*, "The ultimate power in the universe," is trivial. It is a good start. But, in the liberal Jewish world, our pre-Reform ancestors put on special prayer garments, rose for the Sabbath bride, marched with the Torah and let people touch it—virtually kiss it!—as it passed, lit candles—maybe made hand motions, tasted wine, sounded the shofar, chanted and sang, waved the lulav, broke a glass at the end of a wedding, shoveled dirt at a funeral, etc., etc. Physical actions! This has its Christian analogue, of course, with some congregations sitting quietly for most of their worship, while others include kneeling, eating and drinking (the Eucharist), smelling incense, waving arms heavenward, and even speaking in tongues. In recent decades Reform Jewish congregations have been returning to such ritual traditions. Just as it is difficult to think sad thoughts if you cannot frown, so it is difficult not to feel humble before God while bowing your head for a final blessing, or singing *Va'anachnu*. *The emotions are the foundation of our spirituality and the body is the theater of the emotions. So we need to move, to interact with one another, to employ beautiful music along with exalted ideas in our prayers, engaging the mind, of course, but also our senses, to facilitate physically spiritual feelings.*

True confession: I may have been the last Reform rabbi in America to give in to the repeated congregant request that that we rise and face the entrance to the sanctuary to "greet the Sabbath bride" as we finished singing the classic (sixteenth-century kabbalistic lyrics) opening hymn, *L'cha Dodi.* "Empty ritual," I told myself; "the words and music carry the message quite adequately." Nineteenth- and early-twentieth-century Reform Judaism, in revolt against what they perceived as excessive Orthodox ritual, gave up much of the sort of *active* ritual to which I have been alluding. (We were imitating the decorous worship of our Protestant Christian neighbors of the time, so I suspect many a modern Protestant denomination could profitably learn the same lesson today.) In retrospect, I was still in classic Reform rationalist mode while the congregants were hungering for emotion. By now I even enjoy the ritual. As we rise and look expectantly to the door behind us, we are acting out and helping to create, emotionally, our delight at the arrival of Shabbat, and of our being together for it.

Am I saying spirituality is just a trick we play on ourselves, pure emotionalism? The question goes back to the structure of meaning on which we hang our spirituality. Whether you think of God as an omnipresent consciousness, or a more philosophical principal of organization in the universe (order of being, process-in-history, greatest good, etc.), the point is that God is always there though we are not always aware. We are busy and distractible. What is public worship—or for that matter private worship—if not a time to notice the divine?!

Early Reform Jewish thinkers in the nineteenth century were not so much hostile to ritual as they were condescending towards it. They loved a dignified service with fine music and a well-wrought sermon. "Mere ritual" should never distract the community from morality, which mattered far more. Their rebellion made possible shorter, more understandable and intellectually challenging worship. But, with all good intentions, they were too much head and not enough heart. We should beware going to the other extreme. But, by and large, in search of spirituality we have been slowly but surely rebalancing emotion and rationality. Ritual, at home as well as in the synagogue, should include a healthy dose of physicality—and not simply because that is traditional. The physical triggers the emotional and spiritual. An ample dose of ritual was included in the tradition, I have no doubt, because it works.

IF GOD ISN'T LISTENING, WHAT IS GOING ON?

Some readers may be thinking, "Wait! Aren't you the rabbi who told us God is the order of being? Order is not listening! So why would I attend a worship service where, prayer after prayer, we talk to God?" The question is logical, but simplistic. I have written—as have many others, of course—that God, whether understood in more philosophical terms or in traditionalist, personal terms, is beyond anyone's full understanding. All God talk is imprecise and metaphorical.[9] Those who find the personal God metaphor best expresses their experience of holiness, who have a sense that God hears prayers and may respond to requests, should readily find a house of worship where they are comfortable, for God as king/father/judge is the dominant image in classic Jewish and Christian liturgies. Undoubtedly many who come to worship regularly like it that way. We saw in a Pew Research Center study in chapter 1, however, that only 52 percent of Protestant Christians

9. Tillich, *Dynamics of Faith*, 44–48. Gillman, *Sacred Fragments*, 79–80.

and 34 percent of Jews report attending regularly[10] (and I suspect the percentages are actually lower). Even traditional believers appear to be drifting away from public worship. If people truly believed that their presence would lead God to grant the requests in the prayers—for health, for peace, for understanding, for redemption—would they not be more apt to attend? This is the practical side of the problems we sketched in chapter 1, the religiously corrosive effects of theodicy, the scientific worldview and secularism. We live with the benefits of technology and science (air conditioning, inoculations against diseases, computers, etc., etc.). Those we would not willingly go without. Not so, for the majority, with frequent public prayer. Many of us have a faith in God, though not in a God who hears and answers prayers. We are proud of the religious tradition from which we spring, and at life's highs and lows—weddings, funerals and other occasions as we are aware of the sweep of the generations—we want to place our lives in sacred context. We recognize the synagogue, church or other religious center as a vital institution for passing on these traditions. But all these *other* people at worship services seem, at least, to think God is listening to their words. Can we, without self-delusion or hypocrisy, have a meaningful worship experience?

We begin with some easy but partial answers. They are not in themselves sufficient, but nevertheless are an important part of the answer. *First*, not everything that goes on in a worship service is addressed to God. Some of it is specifically addressed to the worshiping community. Certain prayer-like rubrics of the service are more declaration to the congregation than request or praise of God. For Jews an obvious example is the *Shema*, our basic affirmation of faith, addressed to the Jewish people: "Hear, O Israel [*not* "Hear, O God"], *Adonai* is our God, *Adonai* alone. And you shall love *Adonai* your God . . ." (Deut 5:4–5). Christians, similarly, recite various creeds and affirmations of belief. *Second*, music, art and architecture can be inspiring over and above the explicit meanings of the words said or sung. (We may even feel awe in response to cathedrals, paintings, sculptures, the masterpieces of other people's religion!) *Third*, we often study Scripture during worship services, frequently accompanied by classic or modern commentaries, in sermon form or less formal discussion, applying religious wisdom to contemporary life.

Fourth, since anyone can pray privately any time, obviously there is something more to *communal* worship. It fascinates me as a non-Christian to hear the theological and emotional investment that Christians place in "church." It is more than simply the community's worship place, but also an institution founded by Jesus which "the powers of death shall never

10. Pew Forum, "Religious Landscape Study."

conquer" (Matt 16:18).[11] The people Israel is the holy entity for Jews, not the synagogue, important though the synagogue's function is for reinforcing our sense of shared, sacred identity. The most commonly used Hebrew term for synagogue is *beit k'nesset*, literally "house of assembly" or simply "community center." Ideally, that sense of relationship with other Jews is symbolically acted out by attending a synagogue.

Setting aside subtle differences between synagogue, church and other religious gathering places, the fact remains that to have a sense of community there must be a place where people come together to do what is important to them as a group. For a religious community that is going to include religious exercises of some sort. The synagogue was already coming into being for just this purpose even before the Romans destroyed the Jerusalem Temple in the first century. In that same century Paul and other early Christians were developing their new *ecclesia*, from the Greek meaning "assembly" and generally translated as "church," religious institutions to house their private faith. They went first to synagogues (Mark 6:2; Luke 4:16 and 6:6; Acts 13:14–16 and 14:1, etc.), later starting their own—which is to say that a church and a synagogue are functionally the same thing. Each, as just noted, is a community center (*beit k'nesset*, "house of assembly") as well as a place of prayer and religious study (*beit tefillah* and *beit midrash*).

Community in our era has become a value, an ideal in itself, perhaps more so than ever by the nature of anonymous, mass society where many of us do not even know most of our neighbors or live near those with whom we work. Religious institutions are not the only place where we may gather regularly with people with whom we have something important in common. But the religious foundation, the fact that they are intended as places where values are expressed, taught and implemented, and in a multigenerational context at that, gives them the capacity to be far stronger places of mutual caring and support than book clubs, political parties, fraternal orders, youth groups, and the like (indeed, in our time they themselves often sponsor such interest groups). Most also employ specialists, clergy, whose qualifications go beyond worship officiation and religious teaching to organizing and counseling. We go to churches and synagogues for a sense of belonging, to care about others and be cared about ourselves.

By their activities, policies, curricula and choice of liturgies these religious community centers define the religious endeavor in their time. What my Christian clergy colleagues call the "coffee hour" and my rabbinic colleagues and I call the "Oneg Shabbat" ("Joy of the Sabbath," the reception

11. Interpretations vary by denomination, but when Paul, especially in 1 Cor 12:12–31 and Eph 4:1–16, speaks of Christ as the head and people with different gifts as the body, the whole body is generally taken as the church.

before or after the worship service) has become at least as important to most participants as the worship service itself. Many Christians, similarly, do what they call "sharing the peace," pausing in the worship to have people greet and begin to get to know one another. Affinity groups of all sorts (by gender, age, family status—e.g., young marrieds or "empty-nesters," singles, musical abilities, interest in study, etc., etc.) have multiplied in the early twenty-first-century American religious institution. We are very much about overcoming isolation and building community.

Is that enough? It is essential. But enough? Of course not. Building community and caring about one another, and about our society and world (see final chapter), are religious values needed at least as much in our times as in the past. But is not relationship to God, or at least the Holy, the very definition of the religious enterprise? Relatively recent books on community and religious institutions are worthwhile reading, yet their helpful techniques alone are unlikely to end the erosion of participation in synagogues and churches sketched in chapter 1. The author of one of them, worship professor Lawrence Hoffman, memorably suggests that there must be "an actual sense that God [is] present, that worship really is worship, not just socializing."[12]

Those who understand God anthropomorphically (as the personal God who hears their prayers) may be assumed to have that sense of God's presence, or at least to have it when they are in worshipful mood (sometimes, after all, an individual is tired, angry, daydreaming or distracted in some other way, not fully engaged in prayer). Those who think of God more philosophically may find the oft-repeated liturgical metaphor of God as king or father gets in the way of focusing on less tangible metaphors, whether order, truth, process, greatest good or others. The mistake in these cases, though, is focusing on the idea of God as opposed to trying to open oneself (the heart, as it were; sensitivity to the transcendent) to the feeling of being in divine presence. *Worship, in other words, is more about subjective relationship, spirituality, and less about abstract ideas.* Once again, all God talk is metaphorical, and a worshiper should understand that he or she need not be put off by one prayer addressing God as "king" (or "sovereign") and another addressing God as "rock" or "power." None of those, not even "king" for the traditionalist, is literal.

Nevertheless, it is difficult to break ourselves of the habit of thinking of God literally, or almost literally, as ruler/parent/judge, a human-like consciousness. I report this after watching decades of Reform Jewish attempts

12. Hoffman, *Art of Public Prayer*, 80. Also worthwhile for community theme: Wolfson, *Relational Judaism*.

to maintain traditional prayers, which are beloved in many cases, and have been set to equally beloved melodies, while *also* adding less- or non-anthropomorphic prayers to our formal liturgies. *Gates of Prayer* (1975) provided eight services for the eve of Shabbat (plus two more family services).[13] Service 1 is a traditional service of which the next seven are variations. Services 2–8 mostly maintain the Hebrew rubrics of the classic prayer book, but via English meditations and interpretations that vary theologically from a "Religious Naturalism" service to a "Mystical Search" service and even a "Confrontation with Estrangement" service for the doubters. Ironically, between the consistency of the Hebrew and the fact that the descriptions of the varied services were not printed in the book, but only in a commentary printed soon after,[14] rabbis were destined to find that most congregants did not recognize the radical differences in theology from service to service! *Mishkan T'fillah* (2007), therefore, took a different approach. Each traditional Hebrew prayer, and a faithful translation, appears on the right side of each pair of pages, with at least as many theological styles as in *Gates of Prayer* represented in prayers and meditations on the facing left pages.[15] Still, the traditional personal God theism is the (right side) anchor from week to week, varied with (left side) options. So each week congregants hear God, as the more active partner, implored to "sanctify . . . grant . . . purify . . ." in the traditional prayers on the right, which are then enriched on the left with readings placing more stress on human initiative, e.g., "We yearn . . . We seek . . . Be with all who [do various good works]," and so on.[16] I, and no doubt many other rabbis, pointed out such subtleties in sermons and brief commentaries when the prayer book was new. It would be naive to think such lessons were remembered except perhaps by a few regular worshipers. Worse, it would be counterproductive to keep repeating the message that there are traditionalist theological ideas on one side and more philosophical or anthropocentric ones on the other, since—as we just discussed—that would misplace the emphasis on theological abstraction rather than on the primary experience of spirituality.

To put all this differently, while both of these books are excellent, neither will get most secularized modern Jews even to notice, much less embrace, less traditional theology. That would take an ongoing educational effort. People who appreciate the vital importance of divine intangibles enjoy the poetic language of the modernist interpretations, but continue

---

13. *Gates of Prayer*, 117–279.

14. Stern, "Guide to the Services."

15. *Mishkan T'fillah*, ix–xi.

16. *Mishkan T'fillah*, 147 and 193.

to think personal God theism is what they are "supposed to believe," and therefore they think of themselves, very often, as agnostics or atheists. In countless cases, however, they are believers in sacred values which are of the essence religiously. Yet they regard themselves as heretics for their unwillingness to take public worship seriously as communication with God. Public worship could be providing them not miraculous help from the Deity, but spiritual nourishment—moments of transcendence, glimpses of the Divine. The liturgy is probably adequate, but the educational challenge, starting with children but not neglecting adults, is huge.

So it is time to circle back once again to spirituality in order to ask whether those who have their doubts about the personal God metaphor can find a meaningful worship experience. Can a metaphor of God that no one doubts—the structure of being and various "intangibles"—be sufficient for a meaningful worship experience?

SPIRITUALITY IN PUBLIC WORSHIP
EVEN WITHOUT A PERSONAL GOD

What we want of our worship experience, above and beyond all the other good things we have been looking at in this chapter, is a sense of God's presence among us. "A sense of" is a phrase that assumes and accepts our subjectivity. Science strives for accurate description of objective reality. I have argued that for denizens of a scientific and technological age faith must not contradict the facts, but may take us beyond them. Few in our world doubt that there is order to existence. We humans, moreover, with our hardwired sense of order, which enables us to appreciate and often feel awe in the presence of beauty and truth, tenderness but also power, justice, love and so much more, find ourselves from time to time transfixed, uplifted, thrilled, by meaning "out there" in the world and universe. We have seen how that can happen in our experience of nature, of literature and the arts—ideas well as sense perceptions—prompting heartfelt expressions of wonder and gratitude ("Hallelujah!" for the religious; "Wow!" for those who think they are not). All of that is spirituality; the emotion, the enthusiasm, triggered when the objective order and the subjective reaction meet.

We recognize this powerful feeling of transcendence, connection to something awesome and meaningful beyond us, from personal experience, whether we envision God as person-like or as more philosophical. If public worship is well designed and well carried out, it can become an occasion for that triggering of wonder. Returning to the insights of worship professor Lawrence Hoffman, public prayer is enacted; it is staged; it is, in other words, along with being a vehicle for ideas, drama.[17] There is a "set" (some prefer simple surroundings and some prefer grand cathedrals—that is a matter of taste, of what triggers your spirituality), and generally a "script" (the liturgy), even choreography. For most of us—so you need not feel bad if this is you—a deeply felt moment of worship will rarely if ever compete with looking out over Niagara Falls as the sunlight reflects rainbows in the mist. But if your capacity for awe or intellectual excitement is engaged, you may recognize this as analogous to your reaction to Niagara Falls, or to your favorite literary gem or symphony. This too is spirituality, though perhaps not as intense as that which you have felt at waterfalls, births or other peak moments. Recall that in the previous chapter we spoke of revelation in na-ture, in literature and the arts, and in ethics. Natural wonder may be difficult to evoke, though some sanctuaries happen to be located amongst forests or hills or beside bodies of water, and plants and pulpit flowers may help a bit. But literature and the arts are usually of the essence in public worship; so if the prayers and Scripture readings are well chosen and well read, and the music and architecture of a style that touches you (choir? soloist? organ? guitar? soaring ceiling or intimate circle?—these are not right/wrong ques-tions, but matters of taste), these may often be entirely adequate to evoke spiritual response. They will be unlikely to be effective if you are not in the mood and thus unreceptive (no one is every week, much less every day). Ethics are likely to show up, too, via the prayers and readings, and via the sermon. Add long-established symbols of the faith and active participation: the experience can be wondrously effective. *In sum, the point of worship is to join with a community of like-minded seekers, together expressing (prayers), receiving (Scripture and sermon), and feeling (the drama, the art, the ideas) a connection to the community, history and God. Worship services are designed to evoke spirituality.*

As I was about to retire from the full-time congregational rabbinate four years ago, someone in the interfaith clergy group which I have at-tended for years asked how I thought things had changed during my thirty-four-year tenure in one synagogue. It was a subject I had been pondering. The congregation's membership had grown. We had built a beautiful new synagogue building. We had expanded the program and grew the endow-ment. —And fewer people attended Shabbat worship than when I arrived. "Is that package a definition of success?" I asked. My Christian colleagues responded, "Welcome to our world, rabbi!" That is, I interpret, though some churches and synagogues have grown and others shrunk, the main issue or problem is the secular drift of our society, a drift away from spirituality.

17. Hoffman, *Art of Public Prayer*, 161–67.

People are not consciously boycotting, and indeed lots do show up for worship on major holidays and for significant moments in their lives (weddings and births, funerals, bar and bat mitzvahs). I do not believe they are "voting with their feet" against religion, for they are "voting with their checkbooks" by maintaining memberships. They simply do not feel the need for regular public worship. So neither new prayer books from national movements nor changes in musical style or worship schedules can significantly impact the problem. Many have no religious education or only childhood understandings of God and religious living. We have to talk more, not less, about encountering the divine without irrational "leaps of faith." Today's worshipers learned critical thinking at colleges and universities, so the theology we taught them in Sunday school leaves them dubious about a simplistic view of worship (you ask; God ponders, judges and responds). With a more realistic understanding of God, a recognition of their own spirituality both inside and outside synagogues and churches, and education about the multiple agendas of worship, including spirituality, they may well begin to recognize the presence of God in a child's hug, a sunset or an extraordinary moment at a museum or concert—*and* in the sanctuary!

Thus this book. Sensing God in worship will help us feel God in our daily lives. Sensing God in our daily lives will help us feel God in worship.

7

Mitzvah

Is Anything Mandatory?!

Hear, O Israel! The Lord is our God, the Lord alone. You shall love the Lord your God with all your heart and with all your soul and with all your might. Take to heart these instructions with which I command you this day. Impress them upon your children. Recite them when you stay at home and when you are away, when you lie down and when you get up. Bind them as a sign on your hand and let them serve as a symbol on your forehead; inscribe them on the doorposts of your house and on your gates. Thus you shall be reminded to observe all My commandments and to be holy to your God, who brought you out of the land of Egypt to be your God: I, the Lord, am your God.

—Deut 6:4–9 and Num 15:40–41; in classic Jewish liturgy daily

"You shall love the Lord your God . . ." We have seen that we may get a sense of God's reality (revelation) and sometimes of God's presence (spirituality) with a philosophical rather than personal concept of God. Faith remains an important and useful tool as we each move into a future never wholly knowable. Furthermore, public worship and the institutions which house it serve multiple, vital functions for the spiritual uplift of individuals, the creation and maintenance of community, and handing our traditions down from generation to generation. All of that, I suggest, is more than just nice, but less than what our traditions have offered earlier generations. In our Western family of religions—Judaism, Christianity, and Islam—the ideal is for people to feel obligated, *commanded*, to live by our religious teachings: "Take to heart these instructions which I command you this day . . . ." The so-called *Shema* and *V'ahavta* constitute one liturgical unit in nearly every Jewish worship service, proclaiming that we worship the one and only God and show our love and loyalty by following commandments. Especially where ethics are concerned, and to significant degree where ritual is concerned as well, we want people to internalize and be passionate about our religious teachings.

But what does it mean to love God? Does a bacterium in your gut love you? We are tiny, weak and ephemeral; the infinite God spans the universe and eternity. How does one love that which is beyond our full understanding? Stand in awe of, yes. But love? That is a tall order. Fortunately, as we read the passage above, and numerous other passages in the Torah (e.g., Exod 20:6; Lev 26:3–13; Num 15:37–41; Deut 11:1 and 11:13–16), a more pragmatic definition of what it means to love God comes into focus. To love God is to do God's commandments. In the ancient world you showed your devotion to the king by obeying his edicts and paying your taxes, which in a sense is what was going on when you showed your love of the gods or God by obeying laws and presenting sacrifices (remember that polytheists believed the gods actually consumed the sacrifices). This applied to nations as well. Read suzerainty treaties by which small kingdoms like Israel bound themselves to empires such as Assyria, Babylonia and Egypt and you will see lots of flattering words and promises of loyalty.[1] We postbiblical monotheists, most of us, behave towards secular authorities similarly: we follow the laws and pay our obligations. The scale, the numbers of people and the distances involved in realms of influence have in many cases changed. Ironically, though, the political world has not changed so much, and neither has the religious one. Follow the laws, people are often told, and you will be a good Jew—or good Christian or Muslim—or good citizen! Love in the emotional sense may or may not be there, but do the right. Though the terminology is not there in the Hebrew sources, in Greek—and Christian—terms, this love is called *agape*, not *eros*. *Agape* is the sense of willing fulfillment of duty to others, not romantic attachment. Loving God is the non-erotic "love your

---

1. Kugel, *Great Shift*, 178–82.

neighbor as yourself" (Lev 19:18), not the erotic love of "You have captured my heart / With one glance of your eyes, With one coil of your necklace. / How sweet is your love, / My own, my bride!" (Song 4:9b–10a), though (as in English) love in each case is an expression of caring for another. Whether for lover, for neighbor or for God, in love we willingly offer our best selves, our best behavior, to the object of our devotion.

Biblically, then, loving God means taking to heart the instructions which God has *commanded*. Deuteronomy 6, of course, is the chapter immediately following the Decalogue, though it is clear in context that not only the Decalogue, but the whole body of "Instruction—the laws and the rules" (6:1) is to be obeyed, "all His laws and commandments . . ." (6:2). Even in modern, secular America, I suggest, not only traditionalists, but many a liberal Jew or left-wing Protestant Christian, consciously or unconsciously, is committed to obedience to God. The idea of *mitzvah*, commandment, religious duties perceived as obligatory, has been ingrained in us over the centuries. Two examples from my rabbinate may help to make the point.

First: As a congregational rabbi, I have been amused from time to time over the years to find parents dutifully bringing their children to religious school though the parents themselves rarely come for worship, Torah study or other synagogue activities. They want their offspring to be proud of their Jewish identity and—more to the point in this context—they want help inculcating Jewish values. The children should respect learning. They should be helpful to others, including by being charitable. If I push a bit, the question "What other values should they learn?" will generally yield, "The Ten Commandments." These are very secularized people, but they got the message from their parents and grandparents, and their own religious school experience. Being Jewish means more than being part of an ethnic group. "Values" is too bland a word. Certain things they regard as obligatory, commanded by God.

Second: Our synagogue building committee was busily at work on the plans for a new sanctuary. We had agreed that light was to be a unifying artistic motif. Light would stream through clear windows at ground level and stained glass high above. When the ark doors, decorated with a stylized menorah design, were opened, congregants would see the line from Proverbs, "for the commandment is a lamp, and the Torah a light" (Prov 6:23). Just above the ark, as in nearly all synagogues, the *Ner Tamid* ("Eternal Light") would proclaim God's eternal presence. At that focal point, someone at a meeting suggested, we should also display the Ten Commandments. I replied that perhaps we could come up with a more original artistic symbol if we wanted something beyond the ark and Eternal Light. "Everyone uses the Ten Commandments," I said. There was an awkward pause. People looked at me quizzically. "You can't have a sanctuary without the Ten Commandments!" someone said, and others nodded in agreement. While there is no traditional requirement that synagogues be adorned with the tablets or words of the Decalogue, I beat a hasty retreat. If this community of devoted Jews wanted to be symbolically reminded of the *mitzvot* ("commandments") of Judaism every time they entered the sanctuary, no rabbi—certainly not I—would object!

To argue, then, as I have that revelation and spirituality remain even without prophecy is an important first step. Yet if we want a powerful religion the dictates of which we and our children should internalize, not a bland sense of heritage, positive though heritage and identity are, we should strive to agree on which traditional commandments we regard as mandatory for any believer. To put that differently, what do we accept as *mitzvah*? What tangible, concrete actions, ancient or modern (for we have added and interpreted over the ages), do we see as required, and on what basis can we make that claim?

"HEAVIER" AND "LIGHTER" COMMANDMENTS

Be as careful of a light commandment as of a weighty one, for you do not know the given reward of commandments.

—YEHUDA HaNASI, M. *AVOT* 2:1

We recognize in the Mosaic legislation a system of training the Jewish people for its mission during its national life in Palestine, and today we accept as binding only its moral laws, and maintain only such ceremonies as elevate and sanctify our lives, but reject all such as are not adapted to the views and habits of modern civilization.[2]

—"THE PITTSBURGH PLATFORM" OF AMERICAN REFORM JUDAISM, 1885

For many biblical generations, apparently, and virtually all postbiblical generations (not only my congregants on the building committee!), the exalted position of the Ten Commandments, repeated twice in the Torah itself, and the Sinai narrative told and retold in other biblical passages as well, suggest the list of divine commandments should begin there.[3] The story of the revelation at

2. Raphael, ed., *Jews and Judaism*, 204.

3. Moses ascends in Exod 19, and the Decalogue text is then recorded in 20:2–14. A significantly different story of an ascent in which Moses is given "the stone tablets" appears in Exod 24, and the basic story from Exodus is retold in Deut 5, though the

Sinai is myth in the highest sense of the word, wrapping in story a civilization's highest values, among them that we can encounter God and that, having done so, we should behave righteously, following God's ways. For Western religions in particular that means accepting commandments. As symbolic of the whole body of law, the Ten Commandments are treated as "first among equals," but the Torah includes far more, by tradition 613, with the "tree" of Torah growing from those as details are specified for their implementation, and to extend the system of laws/commandments to new situations and technologies.

Thus there are now Jewish laws not only for interpersonal relations (*mitzvot bein adam l'chavero*, commandments between individuals, the tradition calls them), but also for honoring God (*mitzvot bein adam l'makom*, commandments between us and God—prayers, holidays, life cycle ceremonies, dietary and dress laws, etc.). In other words, synagogue and home observance are rooted in the Sinai story as well. Even non-biblical commandments such as kindling lights and drinking wine to inaugurate the Sabbath are introduced with blessings which imply that God gave them (*asher kidshanu b'mitzvotav*; ". . . Who sanctifies us through commandments . . ."), implicitly conferring Sinaitic authority. As postbiblical cultures developed beyond the largely agrarian biblical society, further laws for trade, medicine, marriage—you name it—were needed down through the ages. There are interpretations of commandments which update—*change*—the originals, such as allowing armies to defend themselves and the nation, and physicians to work, on the Sabbath, doing away with polygamy (the Torah assumes it, but times change) and allowing charging interest on loans (the Torah forbids it, but likely had in mind neighbors helping one another when there was a bad crop, not outfitting caravans and ships for world trade). Clearly some commandments are more important than others. But how may we distinguish more from less important ones if they are literally God's word?

With a philosophical God concept this conundrum—what commandments may be modified or even ignored?—is actually a bit easier to address. If God is the order, rules, organization or process of existence, not a conscious being, the principles may be transcendent and meaningful, but the wording and contextual application has to be human, and thus debatable. Not only can there be values conflicts (e.g., the soldier or physician working on the Sabbath to preserve life), but some traditional commandments may not appear logically implied at all by the nature of God! We have dealt earlier with what seem to us to be immoral commandments—genocide, and capital punishment for stubborn and rebellious sons, witches, Sabbath violators, and more. There are

---

mountain is called Horeb, not Sinai, and there are a couple of textual variations in the commandments. In addition to those three accounts echoing one another, Moses, of course, goes back up and receives a second copy of the Decalogue in Exod 34.

also seemingly illogical biblical commandments, such as not mixing wool and flax in the same garment (Deut 22:11, and see also 22:9 and Lev 19:19). The believer in God's personal, verbal revelation must struggle to update seemingly outmoded commandments. The believer in a philosophical God, on the other hand, can assert that moral laws are corollaries of God's nature, and may need modification as our understanding grows over the ages. One would still want a relatively conservative approach to modifying norms, for we are masters of rationalization, and should not allow ourselves to change morality cavalierly. But there was development and change in the past, and it will no doubt continue, however quickly or slowly in different eras.

Morality, then, may be better served by philosophical God concepts. Morality as universal ideal remains mandatory, though applications sometimes need updating. On the other hand, in what sense might ritual laws—prayers, holidays, dietary laws and punishments for violators—be corollaries of God's existence? Petty potentates demand obeisance and gifts. The philosophical God has no personal consciousness to care if you offer a prayer or a sacrifice, and no will to inflict punishment or grant reward. Morally, in other words, there can be drastic consequences if you murder, steal or commit adultery. But ritually, other than psychological impact (not always insignificant!), the consequences of failing to observe a holiday, recite a prescribed prayer or put a *mezuzah* on one's doorpost vary between trivial and non-existent. If the point were simply that there is no anthropomorphic God to "care," the same might be said of moral omissions, but in fact morality has life-and-death consequences and hugely impacts the quality of life in society. Ritual, on the other hand, may be individually satisfying, and help to build personal and communal identity. But ritual and even identity are trivial by compared to morality.

This is not simply a modern observation. In biblical prophetic books there is an implicit debate over the importance of ritual observance, particularly as distinct from ethical mandates. As far back as Amos in the eighth century BCE, the first of the so-called literary prophets (those with books of their prophecy), the prophet presents God as denigrating and seemingly renouncing ritual:

> I loathe, I spurn your festivals,
> I am not appeased by your solemn assemblies.
> If you offer Me burnt offerings—or your meal offerings—
> I will not accept them;
> I will pay no heed
> To your gifts of fatlings.
> Spare Me the sound of your hymns,
> And let me not hear the music of your lutes.

> But let justice well up like water,
> Righteousness like an unfailing stream. (Amos 5:21–23)

A similar denunciation of liturgical pomp and ceremony by and on behalf of sinful people begins the book of Isaiah, the first thirty-nine chapters of which are also by an eighth-century-BCE prophet. His contemporaries are "sinful," "laden with iniquity," "depraved children" who "have forsaken the Lord" (Isa 1:2). This is what God thinks of ritual, and then of morality:

> Bringing oblations is futile,
> Incense is offensive to Me.
> New moon and Sabbath,
> Proclaiming of solemnities,
> Assemblies with iniquity,
> I cannot abide.
> Your new moons and fixed seasons
> Fill Me with loathing;
> They are a burden to Me.
> I cannot endure them. . . .
> (Instead,) Learn to do good.
> Devote yourselves to justice;
> Aid the wronged.
> Uphold the rights of the orphan;
> Defend the cause of the widow.
> (Isa 1:13–14 and 17; see also Jer 7:3–11 and Mic 6:6–8)

Some would say these passages do not condemn ritual, but only the hypocrisy of immorality together with ritual. Either way, there is no denying that preexilic prophets saw ritual as at most a secondary, and morality as the primary, virtue.

Likely the Hebrews in Babylonian exile after the destruction of the first Temple missed the ritual, postexilic prophets such as late-sixth–early-fifth-century-BCE Ezekiel (who happened also to be a priest) spent chapters of painstaking detail specifying what a rebuilt Temple should look like (Ezek 40–44). Not long after the Jerusalem Temple was rebuilt the prophet Malachai indignantly castigates the people for offering second-rate sacrifices (Mal 1:6–14), including, sarcastically, "Just offer it to your governor: Will he accept you? Will he show you favor?—said the Lord of hosts" (Mal 1:8). Ritual, as we saw in chapter 6, is important for giving people a way to act out their faith and identity symbolically, in the process being reminded of their history and values and being touched emotionally and spiritually—hardly trivial matters! But of course being reminded of values is no substitute for individuals living out, and society exemplifying, justice, love, integrity, compassion, and so forth. Simply as a matter of common sense some ethical principles are more important than others, and far more important than ritual piety. Thus murder is worse than theft, protecting and feeding helpless widows and orphans more important than offering sacrifices.

We can worry about *both* "heavy" and "light" commandments, of course, but when push comes to shove common sense determines priorities. We have seen this in biblical times (Amos and Micah above—morality trumping ritual) and it is no less the case postbiblically. In the era of the early rabbis the Mishnah reports that on the fast day of Yom Kippur a pregnant or sick individual may be given food, as may someone with a "ravenous hunger" who seems in danger of passing out. This general principle, which came to be known as *pikuach nefesh*, "[the duty of] saving a life," is immediately extended to Sabbath as well as Yom Kippur violation: "and whenever there is doubt whether life is in danger this overrides the Sabbath." Likewise, if a building collapses and there is reason to suspect someone may be buried in the rubble and might still be alive, it may be cleared away. (*m. Yoma* 8:5–7). Talmudic discussion of the passage not only provides further examples but extends the principle. Break down the door if necessary, for instance, when a child is inadvertently locked in a room on the Sabbath—even if the Sabbath is nearly over! (*b. Yoma* 84b). Again, common sense may sometimes trump legal niceties. In modern terminology we might say that sometimes we follow the spirit rather than the letter of the law. In our context here the point is that, not only with a philosophical God concept, but even with a personal God concept, it need not be heretical to think of ethical commandments as of a higher order than ritual commandments.

MITZVAH: THE FEELING OF WHAT'S MANDATORY, MORALLY

We are tied together in the single garment of destiny, caught in an inescapable network of mutuality. And whatever affects one directly affects all indirectly. For some strange reason I can never be what I ought to be until you are what you ought to be. And you can never be what you ought to be until I am what I ought to be. This is the way God's universe is made; this is the way it is structured.[4]

—M. L. KING JR.

4. King, "Remaining Awake." Delivered March 31, 1968 at the National Cathedral, Washington, DC.

What behaviors, then, are *mandatory* for any decent person, the more so for any religious person aspiring to be not only good, but devoted to God, *holy*? As we have seen, we start with morality (ethics conceptualized systematically). That does not mean society necessarily has a mode of enforcing the ethical in every case. Murder and theft we can prohibit and attempt to punish, but we cannot effectively legislate the routine kindness and integrity that touch us all on a daily basis. There is no way, for instance, to prevent someone from coveting (Exod 20:14 and Deut 5:18), or to enforce "Love your neighbor as yourself" (Lev 19:18).

With philosophical God concepts sometimes we can logically tie ethical norms to the divine order, so that one might say they are at least philosophically mandatory. As we saw in chapter 5, even with the one-celled organism and certainly between individuals and groups of higher species, as they learn to find food, avoid predators and create environments and homes, cooperation is essential for survival and thriving. Cooperation and respect for the rights of others (reciprocal altruism—the "Golden Rule") are required for complex species to thrive. If a race of intelligent beings from a distant galaxy shows up in our realm one of these years, what they will look like is difficult to predict; but we may be reasonably confident that they will cooperate with one another (along with having mastered considerable mathematics and technology), else they would not have had the cultural resources to make the journey. The urge for social harmony is part of the divine order. That does not mean that cooperation cannot also be used in the service of oppression, theft and conquest. At the very least, the food chain demonstrates that the order includes some "law of the jungle" sorts of aggression. Still, *significant levels of cooperation emerge as mandatory to make first life itself, and ultimately civilization, possible.* In our human realm—which evolved out of simian packs and politics, and division of labor in ant colonies and bee hives, before "higher" animals and then human cultures appeared—we dream of greater and greater cooperation making possible larger and larger familial and then communal, national and civilizational groups.

There is, further, morality built into what some wrongly insist is a valueless, meaningless, non-purposeful universe. We more than need, but also trust and normally come to love, the mother who bears us, and then usually the family and often the tribe, community, nation or religious group of which we are a part. *Such trust and love, too, are not just customs, but essential elements of nature if we and other creatures at various levels are to survive and prosper in ever larger and more complex cultures.*

So we begin, as do many animals, with an instinct to bond, which is necessary for an infant's survival into maturity. Early on this becomes a family/non-family, us/them, in-group/out-group habit of thought. But the "us" is extraordinarily elastic. We identify ourselves with larger and larger groups. Think, for example, of your own experience. Most have traveled to different subcultures than you are accustomed to experiencing, in distant corners of the nation and perhaps around the world, and found yourself among people who look different than you—not just skin color, but dress, hairdos, tattoos—and spoke in languages and accents other than your own. You may very well have felt foreign and perhaps ill at ease. Then you ran into someone speaking your language, or otherwise like yourself, and you immediately felt a bond (a fellow American!, a coreligionist!, etc.). The path to world peace appears to be hidden in this capacity: our instinctive us/them thought patterns have stretched over the ages from a sense of oneness with family to analogous bonds with people of towns and cities, to nations of millions and to transnational linguistic, racial, political and religious groupings. To overcome mistrust we simply (well, maybe not so simply; we shall return to this in the next chapter) need a sense of group cohesion with our entire species, the "human family," not just our own smaller groups.

To minimize conflict and maximize harmony, various moral theories have developed over the ages. Various political, religious and philosophic groups advocate differing approaches, though there is much overlap between them. We will probably never achieve unanimity about which system is best. But since we humans, like the plants and animals from which we descended, are part of the evolving order, moral theories which we come up with that work (which, in Darwinian terms, are "adaptive") are themselves manifestations of the order. When values conflict, for instance, Jews tend to stress justice as the highest good, Christians stress love, utilitarians insist on "the greatest good for the greatest number," but others insist on Enlightenment values which defend "unalienable rights" for individuals and minority groups. Life is not as neat as theory, so we fudge, probably wisely so in many cases. In Jewish tradition, when two groups, in good conscience and with Torah-based arguments, advocate opposite sides of a case, the Talmud proclaims that "these and these are the words of the living God." Interestingly, the lesson comes in a narrative in which the schools of Hillel and Shammai debate for three years, until finally a Bat Kol/divine voice makes the declaration, adding that the law should follow the house of Hillel. If both showed pious wisdom, the Talmud continues, why was the decision of the house of Hillel selected? Because they were the more "kindly and modest" (*b. Eruv.* 13:b). Similarly, in both religious and secular argumentation appeals to "the spirit rather than the letter of the law" are common. Emerson famously taught that "a foolish consistency is the hobgoblin of little minds."[5]

---

5. Emerson, "Self-Reliance," 138.

The world and its moral philosophies are not as simple as we might wish. Yet sometimes for our very survival, and consistently for harmonious human societies, morality is indispensable, and thus not neutral but essential—mandatory. If God is the order, and essential to the order are certain values which we can reasonably call ethics, then morality is built into the divine system. As Rabbi Roland Gittlesohn, who called himself a "religious naturalist," regarding God not as a "discrete Supernatural Being" but as the "Spiritual Energy, Essence, Core, or Thrust of the universe," put it: "Mitzvot are not manmade; they inhere within the universe."[6]

RITUAL AS MANDATORY?

For the mitzvah is a lamp,
And the Torah a light.

—PROV 6:23

More than Israel has kept the Sabbath has the Sabbath kept Israel.

—AHAD HA'AM[7]

Our rituals are not, to be sure, unrelated to the divine order. The ancients were well aware of the cycles of the moon and the rotation of the Earth around the sun, and even of water cycles (see Eccl 1:5–7). Likewise in human life, as "one generation goes, another comes" (Eccl 1:4) and we sacralize the life cycle: birth, maturity, marriage, parenthood and death are commonly observed religiously. All these cycles are directly tied to the divine order. Yet the cycles of nature go on with or without our conscious prayers, celebrations and mourning customs. That is not to say ritual is unimportant, but (forgive the pun) it does not hold a candle to morality. Ritual is good for us for all the reasons enumerated in the previous chapter. But morality is a corollary of God's nature; ritual an attempt to refine and improve our own nature. Fail in morality and society and the world may be diminished. Neglect ritual and we diminish only ourselves.

So we will not find a sense of ritual obligation comparable to moral obligation. Scripture's commandments, though placed in God's mouth and ostensibly mandating the observance of Sabbaths and holidays, dietary laws, sacrifices, prayers, historically developed folkways and foods, not to

6. Gittlesohn, "Mitzvah without Miracles," 108.
7. Ha'am, "Shabbat and Zionism," 6.

mention practices for birth and coming of age, marriage and death, and so on, are generally not essential to decent living, though they aide us to appreciate life's blessings. (The exceptions are ritual commandments which shade over into ethical ones, as marriage, for instance, helps regulate sexuality and should ensure male as well as female parenting for each child, or Sabbath commandments that give slaves, laborers and even animals a weekly opportunity to rest.) For the liberal religionist all this is satisfying to have as option and opportunity. But as an option some will do more and some less. Ritual *mitzvot* appeal to our emotional and aesthetic sensibilities. We crave transcendence and spirituality, and in word and deed reaching out to God can provide the gut feeling that our lives matter in community, society and even the larger sweep of history. *So in turning our minds to the divine order, ritual works—which is saying something important! Yet if I miss my religion's biggest holiday this year, have I sinned against God? Not really, for God is not a personality who would be offended, but an order and process which goes inexorably on. I have sinned—if you can call it that—against myself, and against the community, which would be stronger if I participated.* Ethically, moreover, I can continue to try to act in concert with that God whether or not I am in synagogue or church, say grace before a meal or say prescribed words at birth or death.

Thus some do more ritually and some less, and some scarcely anything (even the non-religious tend to come up with marriage and death rituals, with or without recourse to God, as they endeavor to appreciate values and memories, and thus savor the significance of the moment). Rituals survive in our more secular culture because—in Darwinian terms again—they work. They are adaptive in that they help us see life's blessings more clearly and cope with its challenges, appreciating the importance of the families, communities and values on which, as social and emotional creatures, we depend for guidance and support.

There is reason to doubt whether communal institutions and values could survive without our finding ways to act out our convictions, and in the process to think about where we have come from as religious communities, where we hope we and the world are going and how each of us, personally, fits in. That is what we are doing regardless of our God concept. Rituals, moreover, are often beautiful and enjoyable. But if I miss Shavuot this year (as, believe me, the vast majority of American Jews will), though it is commanded in Scripture (Exod 34:22; Lev 23:15–21; Num 28:26–31; and Deut 16:9–12)[8] and symbolizes nothing less than the revelation of God to

8. The number of references—and there are more which do not use the name Shavuot ("Weeks")—speaks to the importance of this harvest festival, which postbiblical generations magnified even further with the Sinai symbolism. See Jacobs, "Shavuot,"

Israel, the loss, as noted above, is only to me and us, not to God. *Ritual is a help in recognizing the divine order, but not a corollary of the divine order. It is instrumental, not essential.*

Let's pursue that for a minute before turning more directly to the question of how, if at all, ritual can be seen as mandatory. I am saddened when a synagogue member tells me he is going on a fishing trip over Yom Kippur. I can "guilt" him with not supporting his fellow congregants, and tell him in all sincerity that he is missing important spiritual opportunities. But when he says he always feels closest to God in the wilderness, and that he knows he can repent any day, I cannot in good conscience tell him God will punish him (I *can* say his children will see him; but they probably already know how serious as a Jew he is or is not). I am not, to be sure, arguing against the value of prayer, ritual, repentance or setting a good example for the next generation, merely honestly distinguishing between the authority, the "mandatoriness," of moral and ritual *mitzvot*. It would be an offense against all that is holy if he were to abandon or abuse his loved ones or burn down the synagogue. But it is mostly his own loss, and there may even be some compensatory gains, if he goes fishing with his buddies instead of going to worship services.

Millions of us do, of course, highly value the survival of our own religious community, and if for countless people in our communities secularism (e.g., going fishing, or to work, on a Sabbath or holiday) eclipses the most basic of rituals, that weakens the community (in the first chapter, you will recall, we saw that synagogue and church affiliation rates, and participation rates among the affiliated, are dramatically down). So if God does not literally require a given ritual action, is there some other sense in which moderns might feel *commanded* to observe ritual?

Years ago General Motors had a series of advertisements intended to sell cars. A peppy song declared, "We love baseball, hotdogs, apple pie and Chevrolet!" as the picture portrayed smiling, relaxing people. It was the affect, the warm smiling pictures and our own nostalgic associations, that the company hoped would lead us to a Chevrolet dealer when we wanted a new automobile—not the miles per gallon, horsepower, or other mechanical aspects the product had to offer. Emotional appeal first; then a salesman could pitch the car's functionality. It was to such aspects of culture, in his case Jewish culture, to which Mordecai Kaplan pointed when he worried, in his 1934 book, *Judaism as a Civilization*, that his fellow Jews were drifting away from Judaism, and sought a rationale to stem the tide. According to Kaplan, each civilization—in the sense of large-group culture passed down through many

---

13 20.

generations—has its "*sancta*," the facets which the person who becomes a part of it recognizes as his or her own. These elements, including but not limited to ritual, "objects, persons, places, events, days, etc., and specific codes of laws, customs and morals," exist to turn the minds of individual members of the group to the group. Every culture has such "*sancta*."[9] To be a Jew is to be personally involved with these *sancta*. First there is a sense of belonging to the group, then one goes on to its beliefs. The sense of religious obligation derives from the civilization, the collective group, not from God. The Orthodox claim authority for religious obligation comes from divine revelation, and the "Reformist" "rejoices to find in Judaism truths of universal application, the unity of God, the brotherhood of man, the supremacy of righteousness." But actually a member of a unique civilization "realizes that the force of a social heritage lies not in its abstract and universal values, but in its individuality, in its being unalterably itself, and no other."[10] So for Kaplan God, sacred texts and ritual discipline, as well as moral behavior, are all on the list of *sancta*. As Kaplan (you may recall) believed that God was a process working for good or for salvation in history, not a conscious being, he thus solved, to the satisfaction of many Jews of his time, the question of how traditional ritual could be experienced as commanded, *mitzvah*, without a personal God commander. The whole tradition commands. History commands. Though God and morality are items on the list of *sancta*, the "commander" is the evolving civilization of the Jewish people (an argument which could readily apply in other religious cultures too).

The *mitzvot*, even the moral and certainly the ritual, have evolved over time and will continue to do so. Kaplan himself knowingly contributed to the evolution of beliefs and rituals (e.g., denying that the universal God had a single "chosen people," and providing a bat mitzvah for his daughter when previously only males had such a coming-of-age ceremony). So Kaplan and his followers (who call themselves Reconstructionists and have created a Jewish denomination) have not created a single, authoritative set of mandatory *mitzvot*. On the communal level, once one sees, not God's will, but rather the practice of the community over time as the shaper of the religious culture, continued development is as natural as it is inevitable. On the individual level, given all the positive aspects of ritual observance, what each must do is find some set of rituals which work for him or her—not a predetermined list, though denominational guidance and thus collective wisdom are found to be helpful. The theoretical possibility of believing theologically but doing nothing ritually will rarely be invoked, for ritual provides

9. Kaplan, *Judaism as a Civilization*, 320 and 323.

10. Kaplan, *Judaism as a Civilization*, 184.

the emotional glue to hold families together and enrich individuals with spiritual experience. Ritual further entails the positive theological gain of reminding ritual participants of the ideas being enacted and, ideally, in the process cementing the conviction that life is meaningful and sacred despite suffering and death.

In Reform Judaism's late-twentieth- and now twenty-first-century re-appropriation of traditional ritual, Kaplan's influence is manifest ("Why are you doing that?" "Because it makes me feel Jewish!"—that is, not because God commands it, but because it makes us feel authentic.) Kaplan taught for many years at Conservative's Jewish Theological Seminary, and I hear essentially the same answer from Conservative Jews who often keep dietary laws at home but feel free to ignore them when eating out. They are doing so for a sense of personal authenticity as heirs to the tradition, not in obedience to God. Lacking a conscious, demanding God as the source of revelation, this rabbi will not tell a member of the community that he or she is a sinner for not observing any given ritual. *What I can and do say is that a measure of ritual discipline is mandatory for anyone who respects a religious culture. The accumulated weight of tradition demands—commands—that the adherent of any religious culture—mine for me, others for them—find those rituals which evoke their spirituality individually and keep the community alive and vital collectively.*

In sum, it is difficult for society to enforce morality, and impossible to impose piety. Still, in a world in which there is a God—an order moving the inanimate towards life, and life towards harmony, intelligence and survival—our conscious, self-aware species should feel obligation, a sense of *mitzvah*, to respect one another and the world, and to add to the store of divine intangibles whenever possible. *Moral mitzvot are corollaries of the nature of God. Ritual mitzvot are necessary to keep us and future generations emotionally as well as intellectually loyal to God and the tradition, the "civilization," of which we are heirs. If we neglect either the moral or the ritual, we spiritually impoverish ourselves and risk our collective future.*

8

The Importance of the
Messiah Who Isn't Coming

*Mendel: Rabbi, we've been waiting for the Messiah all our lives.
Wouldn't this be a good time for him to come?*

*Rabbi: We'll have to wait for him someplace else. Meanwhile, let's
start packing.*

—FROM *FIDDLER ON THE ROOF*
(AS THE PEOPLE ARE BEING EXPELLED FROM THEIR HOMES)[1]

Imagine that you and I have gone to do an exercise in a large open area
somewhere, and we are standing together. Behind us is a mountain, off to
our right a chasm, and to the left a plain stretches as far as the eye can see.
I say to you, "Take three steps to the left," and you do. Then I ask, "Do you
feel closer now?" You look back quizzically. "Closer to what?" you ask. "To
where you should go," I answer, which does not clear up your confusion.
The situation would be no clearer had I said to go right, or to begin climbing the mountain. Unless you know the goal, all motion is random. Goals

---

1. Stein, *Fiddler on the Roof*, 142.

give direction, purpose, as well as a sense of challenge as we ponder them, and satisfaction or frustration as we succeed or fail in achieving them. This is true for the geographic goal of this simple exercise, and no less true for other goals—career goals, learning to play the piano, the search for friendship and love, or the yearning for a just society or world peace. Goals shape as well as reflect our values, and in the process guide our lives. Pursuing honors, riches or love, developing talents, sensing God's presence, devoting oneself to causes—nation, peace, improving the lot of others, etc.: some goals will be largely self-chosen, and others, consciously or unconsciously, will be adopted from our cultures. But goals there must be, after which purpose and meaning enter our lives.

That is what belief in a Messiah and messianism, first in Judaism and then Christianity, is all about. So in this final chapter we shall first look at the context out of which messianism grew, the better to define it. Then we will consider how modern believers with a non-miraculous, philosophical rather than personal God concept can deal with it.

AROUND AND AROUND AND AROUND?

Many peoples even today picture both the natural world and their own lives as proceeding in cycles, and likely more did in the ancient world. The sun rises and sets each day, the moon goes through its monthly phases and season follows season annually. Life too has its cyclical aspects. We are born, mature, reproduce and die, generation after generation. And early farmers no less than modern ones saw animals and plants follow the same pattern. Biblical generations, moreover, understood sexuality as our human echo of nature, women's bodies following monthly cycles and men planting their "seed" where they hoped it would grow into new life. The heavens were cyclical as well, not only the lunar cycle, but also constellations appearing, moving across the skies and disappearing, only to return the next year. We see a Hebrew version of this in chapter 1 of the biblical book of Ecclesiastes, where, interestingly, its author misunderstood the wind, but partially figured out the water cycle:

> One generation goes, another comes,
> But the earth remains the same forever.
> The sun rises, and the sun sets—
> And glides back to where it rises.
> Southward blowing,
> Turning northward,
> Ever turning blows the wind,

On its rounds the wind returns.
All streams flow to the sea,
Yet the sea is never full;
To the place [from] which they flow
The streams flow back again. (Eccl 1:4–7)

It was not only the author of Ecclesiastes, of course, who thought the world operated cyclically. Hinduism, Buddhism, and Jainism abound in wheels of life representing human life or the whole universe (look up mandala or bhavacakra online, for instance, for ample and often beautiful illustrations). Pre-Socratic philosopher Anaximander in the fifth century BCE spoke of the cyclical occurrence of worlds, which "may very well be the original source of the modern cyclical theory of history." Likewise, the Stoic school of Greek philosophy in the fourth century BCE and beyond took up the theme of eternal recurrence.[2] Thomas Cahill, in his 1998 bestseller, *The Gifts of the Jews*, declares Abram's going forth from Mesopotamia a radical act. In an age when everyone saw life and the world as cyclical and thus un-changing, he was to leave the Sumerian civilization and do something new, go to the land God would show him and become father to a new people:

> On every continent, in every society, Avram would have been given the same advice that wise men as diverse as Hericlitus, Lao-Tsu, and Siddhartha would one day give their followers: do not journey but sit; compose yourself by the river of life, medi-tate on its ceaseless and meaningless flow–on all that is past or passing or to come–until you have absorbed the pattern and have come to peace with the Great Wheel and with your own death and the death of all things in the corruptible sphere.[3]

Cahill may exaggerate some by insisting that everyone prior to Abram would have agreed that life and the world were cyclical and therefore nothing new could ever happen. Yet the religious view of the Abrahamic traditions, Juda-ism and then Christianity and Islam, is indeed radical. The Hebrew Bible presents not only a beginning, but an end-time goal. Now we can think of history as linear, as leading somewhere and not just going 'round and 'round. It begins with creation and will ultimately lead to some different and better state, which is the *messianic* goal.

But did we not just see a cyclical view of reality in Ecclesiastes, which is to say in the Bible? Yes, and Ecclesiastes says much more along these lines as it insists that "there is nothing new under the sun" (1:9) and thus that all

2. Thilly and Wood, *History of Philosophy*, see Anaximander, 25, and Stoics, 135.
3. Cahill, *Gifts of the Jews*, 64.

our efforts to attain what people strive for—riches, wisdom and pleasures of all sorts—are vain "striving after wind" (1:14 and eight more times through the book). Follow God's commandments, of course (12:13), yet "sometimes a good man perishes in spite of his goodness, and sometimes a wicked one endures in spite of his wickedness. So don't overdo goodness and don't act the wise man to excess" (7:15–16). This pessimistic view of life is an eternal temptation (stop trying so hard; it will not work!). We do often act on vain, misplaced priorities. Yet not only has physical reality developed, and life evolved, from simpler to more complex, but so have human understanding and behavior—which leads to cultural evolution. Over the ages we have created new technologies—writing, medicine, architecture, etc.—and myriads of ways of organizing our thoughts and societies. Think of the insistence in Ecclesiastes that "all is futile and pursuit of wind" as the Hebrew Bible's minority report. The majority view, as we shall see, wants us to strive to make ourselves and the world better.

But we are getting ahead of ourselves. It is time to go back and define the Abrahamic religions' messianism and messianic goal or goals.

WHAT IS A MESSIAH?

The Hebrew word *messiah* translates as "anointed one." In biblical society they inaugurated the service of a king or high priest by anointing him with oil (think olive oil, perhaps with fragrant spices). There are numerous references to God promising that David's dynasty would go on forever (most notably 2 Sam 7:11–16), and David, for all his faults, in the folk imagination was hailed as the great warrior and leader who united the kingdom, moved his capital to Jerusalem and wanted to build a temple there (which Solomon, as Davidic heir, did). David was also renowned as the pious author of psalms, and was truly repentant when his sins were pointed out to him (2 Sam 11–12, especially 12:13–14). So when, despite foreign domination from time to time, and exile to Babylon, Hebrews dreamed of return to the land and restoration of national glory, it was natural to dream of a Davidic descendant restoring independence and former glory. They sometimes referred to this imagined leader as *messiah*, but in this early context that simply meant a Davidic, anointed king. In the final verses of Amos (eighth century BCE) the prophet predicts that God will reestablish "the fallen booth of David," and the nation will again rule surrounding peoples. There will be enduring prosperity, "[a]nd I will plant them on their soil, / Nevermore to be uprooted, / From the soil I have given them / —said the Lord your God" (Amos 9:11–15; see also eighth-century-BCE Hos 3:4–5).

It will then be plain, in the words of Psalm 18:50, that God "keeps faith with [or "performs loving-kindness for"] his anointed [*meshi'cho*, "His messiah"], / with David and his offspring forever." Such passages imagine a great Davidic leader, to be sure, but there is little if anything supernatural in the concept—God is the dispenser of all blessings, after all, including the king's.

Once people dream, however, why not dream bigger? In Isaiah 11 (eighth century BCE) "a shoot shall grow out of the stump of Jesse [David's father]" and "the spirit of the Lord shall alight upon him." Wonders well beyond the political will ensue. Through this anointed king God's spirit will be manifest in many ways:

> A spirit of wisdom and insight,
> A spirit of counsel and valor,
> A spirit of devotion and reverence for the Lord.
> He shall sense the truth by his reverence for the Lord;
> He shall not judge by what his eyes behold,
> Nor decide by what his ears perceive.
> Thus he shall judge the poor with equity
> And decide with justice for the lowly of the land.
> He shall strike down a land with the rod of his mouth
> And slay the wicked with the breath of his lips.
> Justice shall be the girdle of his loins,
> And faithfulness the girdle of his waist.
> The wolf shall dwell with the lamb,
> The leopard lie down with the kid;
> The calf, the beast of prey, and the fatling together,
> With a little boy to herd them. . . .
> In all of My sacred mount
> Nothing evil or vile shall be done;
> For the land shall be filled with devotion to the Lord
> As waters cover the sea. (Isa 11:1–9)

In such passages (see also Isa 9, especially 9:5–6) we see the "anointed one" beginning to be not only wise, but miraculously effective in bringing about justice and peace. Neil Gillman, long-time professor of Jewish philosophy at the Jewish Theological Seminary, goes so far as to suggest that the reign of this Davidic king will be "justice incarnate."[4]

Nor are we finished with glorious dreams! In Ezekiel 37 (sixth century BCE) the Davidic king is destined to reunite the northern and southern kingdoms; everyone will faithfully obey God's commandments; and God will "take the Israelite people from among the nations they have gone to,

---

4. Gillman, *Sacred Fragments*, 252.

and gather them from every quarter, and bring them to their own land"
(Ezek 37:21). "[T]hey and their children's children shall dwell there forever,
with my servant David as their prince for all time. I will make a covenant of
friendship with them for all time—it shall be an everlasting covenant with
them—I will establish them and multiply them, and I will place My Sanctuary among them forever . . ." (Ezek 37:25–26).

Perhaps as a frustrated reaction to the failure of such a political savior
to arrive, bringing eternal peace and independence, postbiblically the messianic dream takes on phantasmagorical elements. The dead in the land of
Israel would be resurrected! Resurrection of the dead is hinted at, but seems
mostly metaphorical in most of the Hebrew Bible (as in Ezekiel's chapter
on the valley of the bones, Ezek 37). In late biblical times, under oppres-
sive regimes, the notion of the dead literally coming back to life to receive
their just reward or punishment appears in the third-century-BCE book of
Daniel (Dan 12:1–3). Under Rome a couple of centuries later the folk and
rabbinic imagination joined the expected resurrection with the expected
coming of the Messiah. This was controversial at first. Sadducees (first century CE) denied resurrection even as the rabbis proclaimed in the Mishnah
(first to third century CE) that every Jew will have a share in the world to
come—except for various heretics, including first of all those who deny that
the dead will be resurrected (*m. Sanh.* 10:1).

Under oppression in general, and especially after its association with
another end-time dream, the coming of the Messiah, it is not difficult to
imagine the logic of bodily resurrection. Those suffering under the boot of
oppressors in Daniel's time, and later under Rome, might well have asked
themselves, "Why should we, and our parents and grandparents, after keeping the faith all these years, not enjoy the great new age too? It isn't fair!"
They found comfort and reassurance in the idea that a king Messiah would
lead them to renewed independence, at which time not only the living, but
the dead, resurrected, would enjoy the messianic world. First the dead in
the land of Israel would return to life. Then even the dead outside the land
would revive and roll through underground passages to *eretz yisraeyl* for the
glorious reward (*Midr. Rab., Exod. Rab.* 96:5)! Over the centuries and down
to our own era, some Jews have arranged to be transported to Jerusalem for
burial, or at least to be interred with a bag of Jerusalem soil in their caskets,
so they can be resurrected right away, without the subterranean journey,
when the Messiah comes. In the messianic kingdom there will be peace and
plenty, justice and piety, and from there this utopian vision will spread to
all the world.

WHEN WILL THE MESSIAH ARRIVE?

This was the Jewish dream, rooted in biblical texts but extended far beyond. Then the Messiah failed to arrive—or at least has not arrived yet! There was disagreement—one might even go so far as to say confusion—over what was reasonable to expect. In a wonderful tale in the Gemarrah (third-to-sixth-century-CE commentary on the Mishnah)[5] Rabbi Joshua ben Levi, frustrated that the Messiah has not arrived, is assured by none other than the prophet Elijah[6] that the Messiah is here already, wrapping bandages around the wounds of lepers at the gates of Rome. Rabbi Joshua goes to him and asks when he will come. "Today!" the Messiah answers. The rabbi returns to Elijah, but is again upset that the redemption has not occurred. "He lied!" protests Rabbi Joshua. At which Elijah explains, "This is what he said to you, 'Today—if you will hearken to His voice'" (Ps 95:7). That is, when we are righteous enough the Messiah, who is always ready, will become visible (*b. Sanh.* 98a). Other passages in the same Talmudic discussion, however, suggest that when things get so bad in our realm that God cannot stand it any longer, God will send the Messiah (*b. Sanh.* 97a).

Which is it? Will God send the Messiah when things are wonderful or when they are horrible? Between those extremes, a charming but world-weary passage in Avot de Rabbi Natan advises, "If you should happen to be holding a sapling in your hand when they tell you the Messiah has arrived, first plant the sapling and then go out to greet the Messiah" (*Avot R. Nat.*, ed B, 31). When Maimonides wrote his famous "Thirteen Principles of Faith," the twelfth declared, "I believe with perfect faith in the coming of the Messiah; and, though he tarry, I will wait daily for him."[7] Had people in Maimonides' twelfth century not been expressing doubts, the phrase "and though he tarry" would not have been necessary encouragement.

Nearly a thousand years later the epigraph at the beginning of this chapter similarly reflects impatience as the messianic promise, generation after generation, went unrealized. The author of the script for *Fiddler on the Roof*, which was based loosely on Sholem Aleichem's Tevye the Diaryman stories, actually softened the bitter frustration in the original. There Tevye, musing

5. Printed together they comprise a Talmud.

6. Rabbinic lore, taking off from the story in 2 Kgs 2 of Elijah not dying as ordinary mortals do, but being taken to heaven in a whirlwind (2:11), imagines Elijah coming back from time to time to check how Jews are faring, and thus whether or not it is time for the Messiah to arrive. See also Mal 3, which speaks of a final, fearsome day of judgement, and says that Elijah will arrive before that day and reconcile parents and children. All of this becomes associated in rabbinic-era lore with the arrival of the Messiah, and Elijah becomes the herald of the Messiah.

7. Hertz, *Authorized Daily Prayer Book*, 255.

on Jewish suffering in the "topsy-turvy" world of Czarist Russia, where he and his fellow Jews suffer poverty, and the latest antisemitic insult is the trial of Mendel Beiliss (1913), who was brought up on the absurd charge of using the blood of a Christian child to make Passover matzah, thinks:

> How could this be happening? . . . How could it be possible, in these times, in such a clever world full of such smart people! And where was God, the old Jewish God? Why was he silent? How could he allow such a thing? . . . And why does the Messiah not come? Ay, I thought, wouldn't it be wonderful if the Messiah were to come down right now riding on his white horse! That would be a fine thing! Never has he been so badly needed by our Jewish brethren as now. . . .

At just that moment Tevye looks up and finds a man approaching his door on a white horse! But it is the Russian constable, who has come to tell him and the rest of the Jews that they must leave their homes and village, sell what they can and evacuate within three days.[8]

With such modernist doubts even in more tradition-minded Eastern Europe, it is no wonder that Reform Judaism, with rationalist zeal in nineteenth-century central Europe and America, gave up on the arrival of a Messiah. But even they held on to the idea of a messianic age. American Reform rabbis, in "The Pittsburgh Platform" of 1885, rejected belief in "bodily resurrection and in Gehenna and Eden (Hell and Paradise)." They immediately went on to affirm, however, that "[w]e recognize, in the modern era of universal culture of heart and intellect, the approaching of the realization of Israel's great Messianic hope for the establishment of truth, justice, and peace among all men."[9] Even without the Messiah, messianism remained the goal! Reformers declared the "Mission of Israel" (meaning the Jewish people; there would not be a state by that name until 1948) was to work with its "daughter religions," Christianity and Islam, and indeed with all people of conscience, to achieve the messianic age.

Traditionalist Jews still pray for the Messiah to arrive, but especially after the Holocaust dubious moderns might be forgiven for the corrosive thought that he is not coming. What about the messianic age *sans* the individual Messiah? In the years of my rabbinate I have seen the term "Mission of Israel" all but disappear from Jewish rhetoric, but only to be replaced by the term *tikun olam*, a traditional term meaning "perfecting the world." The former suggests, perhaps naively,[10] that Jews (albeit with allies) might *as a*

8. Aleichem, *Tevye the Dairyman*, 120–21.

9. Raphael, *Jews and Judaism*, 204.

10. Silver, "Lover's Quarrel." Silver argued that, while it may have been good

group lead the world to righteousness and peace, while the latter focuses more on what each *individual*, Jewish or otherwise, can do to effect *tikun olam*, making the world, a bit at a time, more perfect. In a world replete with threats to humanity's survival, and brimming with hatreds (racial, religious, national, gender, etc.), that remains a bold goal. The saving grace here is that we have seen the theological concept of Messiah as a growing myth practically from the start. Myth: by now we know that myths carry a culture's highest values without needing to be valid as history or science. *Of course the Messiah is not literally coming, nor are human beings so perfectible that we will ever fully achieve a utopian messianic dream. But we can do a lot better than we are doing now.*

A quick look at the Christian twist on Jewish messianism will, not surprisingly, reveal both dramatic differences and important links. Just as the rabbinic tradition reinterpreted messianism to make suffering under the boot of Rome, and later others, more tolerable, early Christians reinterpreted the messianic idea. There was no need to despair over suffering and injustice. The Messiah, they said, had already arrived! But the messianic task was not the political redemption Jews awaited, throwing off foreign domination and bringing justice and peace. Regardless of who ruled, the messianic goal was spiritual redemption. "Render therefore unto Caesar what is Caesar's, and to God the things that are God's" (Matt 22:21). Both rabbinic Jews and early Christians (also mostly Jews, recall) of the time, probably under Hellenistic influence, had begun to think about souls surviving the death of the body, an idea only hinted at in the Hebrew Bible, but much discussed by the early rabbis as well as the early church.[11] The reward for keeping the faith need not be redemption in this life, but could be awareness of spiritual redemption now while the actual reward was postponed to the next life.

A full discussion of how all this developed would take us far from the main line of thought here. We may note, though, that just as Jews shared at least some of the Christian emphasis on individual immortality, Christians shared at least some of the Jewish emphasis on political peace and harmony. With first Roman cruelty and oppression to deal with, and later that of others, both faith communities had to answer the question of what had become of the prophetic promise of peace—Isaiah's wolf dwelling with the lamb and leopard lying down with the kid quoted above, and many other such visions. We spoke of the postbiblical blossoming of wondrous ideas about

---

rhetoric, it has never been good theology to think the relatively small Jewish people could lead the entire world to redemption.

11. For Hellenistic thought and Christianity as sources for the idea of the immortality of the soul, see "The Soul Which Thou Hast Given unto Me?" in Mecklenburger, *Our Religious Brains*, 61–68.

the Messiah. Jesus, declared the long-awaited Messiah, came to be regarded as more than a human "anointed one" sent by God, but as an incarnation of God. Through faith an individual could know spiritual peace now, and the promise of life everlasting in heaven—brutal though Rome might be. Christianity, in this way, significantly spiritualized messianism. Still, Jesus not only promised peace, but preached and modeled this-worldly compassion and humility, and devotion to the poor, weak and helpless. "As you did to one of the least of these my brethren, you did to me" (Matt 25:40). Worldly goodness, it was promised, was a way of serving God which would be rewarded in heaven. As Jews awaited the Messiah for redemption in this world, the church came to expect a *second* coming when the this-worldly part of the messianic promise would be fulfilled. Islam would later deny Jesus was an incarnation, but nonetheless regard him as an "anointed one," a Messiah who would return to earth as part of a final judgement.

Summing up for a moment: out of a world in which the path of wisdom was often understood as learning to adapt to the evils of life and history, the Abrahamic religions—first Judaism, then Christianity and Islam—came up with a sublime goal towards which each and all may work. The righteous would one day enjoy world peace, harmony and other divine intangibles which make life worthwhile—justice, beauty, truth, love, compassion and more. As we have discussed throughout this volume, a philosophical God does not take conscious actions—including sending a Messiah. Nevertheless, the very reality of an order of being, and of its divine intangibles, and thus our ability within that order to envision and work towards a better world, gives us the potential to set reasoned goals, grounded in our experience, as steps towards the ideal world. Even if humanity never gets there, and even without physical resurrection, we know what we ought to strive for. The messianic era is more even than Gillman's "justice incarnate." *The Messiah, and thus messianism, represent our fondest hopes incarnate, the world perfected in human history.*

THE HARDWIRED "US AND THEM"

Have we not all one Father? Did not one God create us? Why do we break faith with one another, profaning the covenant of our ancestors?

—MAL 2:10

A child is born. Parents, relatives on both sides and close friends are all thrilled. Thanks at least in part to hormones released in the mother's brain in the birth process, the mother almost immediately wants to hold and cuddle the new child. She will nurse and change this little person, rock her, comfort her, laugh with her, respond to the baby's endless whims. If the father is present, he will likely develop similar bonds. Family and friends too, and even many total strangers, will find the baby adorable. "So little!" they will say. "So cute!" Much of this is hardwired behavior, the result of genetics and hormones.[12] We see such instinctive and often tender caregiving in many of our pets, and with the birds outside the bedroom window sitting on the nest and later flying back and forth with food.[13] But insects lay their eggs and disappear. Guppies and various other animals seem to lack any parental behavior, and may enjoy newborns for breakfast![14] So our human reactions to parenthood are not inevitable, but the result of evolution. In the mid-twentieth century psychologists battled over how important parental hugging and cuddling were for infants. The experiments on monkeys of the University of Wisconsin's Dr. Harry Harlow (infant monkeys preferred a cloth-covered wire "mother" to the wire figure alone even when milk was available only from the latter), and studies of infants in orphanages, who even with proper nutrition and medical care "failed to thrive" and often died if not regularly touched, mostly ended the debate.[15] The hardwired need in both parents and children for relationship—we can reasonably call it love—develops from both sides, from the child as well as the mother or other caregivers.

This is a beautiful thing. Our need for physical and psychological relationship with special others continues throughout our life cycle. Yet it appears also to be the root of various problems, which can be dealt with but not eliminated. In a crowd of little ones, recently, I witnessed a toddler grab his mother's hand and declare proudly, "*My* Mommy!" He would adjust, but was likely in for some rough weeks when the pregnant mother delivered a competitor for her attention. We are each born with various survival mechanisms and learn others. Ideally we find that family will take care of us, and can be trusted to have our well-being in mind in unfamiliar or otherwise threatening situations. As we grow we learn about the role of teachers, and perhaps of neighbors. We are social creatures who come to trust, and in turn to feel some obligation towards, first family and then other groups, larger and larger circles of folks around us. There is a flip side to all this trusting,

---

12. Churchland, *Braintrust*, 33–34.

13. De Waal calls birds "doting parents" in Waal, *Bonobo and the Atheist*, 7.

14. Though few reptiles show parental instincts, de Waal finds alligators a notable exception. Waal, *Bonobo and the Atheist*, 7.

15. Lewis et al., *General Theory of Love*, 69–72; Waal, *Age of Empathy*, 11–13.

however. It may be scary to go outside those familiar groups, though of course learning to meet new people and groups is part of growing up. Still, seeing our world in us/them terms comes naturally.

The problem, then, is that we quickly learn to trust familiar people and mistrust others. "Don't go with strangers!" we rightly warn our children. And whom do we meet first? By and large we meet those with whom we have things in common—family, of course, and then neighbors and community members. Early on we will find ourselves more comfortable with people who look like us, speak our language, share attitudes and beliefs with us—larger and larger us/them groups. *"Like us" is not a bad thing per se; we need a sense of belonging and comfort. But each "us" implies a "them," the ones with whom we are not so comfortable and who might even want to harm us.* In schools, and later in neighborhoods and cities, we will form cliques and affinity groups of all sorts. Even if we rarely feel mistreated by others, and certainly if we do, consciously or unconsciously the roots of racism, sexism, classism, chauvinism and hatreds of all sorts become part of us.

In addition—returning to hardwired, instinctual behaviors—we are naturally selfish, wanting our food first, the best toy (which actually may only look better because that other kid picked it up first) and one day the most desirable boyfriend or girlfriend. We can learn to share, learn when competition is part of the game and when it is just selfish, and even learn one day to feel responsible for others (first, of course, our own families, then our city, country or religious group, and so on—the same roughly concentric circles going out from the self in the center). Our brains, the anthropologists say, evolved for us to live in small groups of 150 or so people; we can't even keep track of, let alone come to know well, too many more than that individually.[16]

Still, we are also hardwired for compassion, feeling the pain of others. When one baby in a hospital nursery begins to cry, soon others join in. And at the very least we feel bad for people, and often even animals, whom we see mistreated, or suffering pain. Every culture has a version of what psychologists call "reciprocal altruism" and religions preach as "the Golden Rule."[17] These are universals too, instincts which often motivate us to care not only for "us" but even for "them." Our situation, in other words, is not at all hopeless. But it is easier to teach our offspring to care for themselves and their in-group circles than to care about, and be generous towards, strangers.

---

16. Dunbar, *How Many Friends*, 21–34; or see Gladwell, *Tipping Point*, 175–81.

17. Hauser, *Moral Minds*, 357–418; Haidt, *Happiness Hypothesis*, 45–58.

Would we be better off had evolution programmed us to regard all people, regardless of physical differences (e.g., race, gender) or cultural differences (e.g., family, nation, religion, language), as the same? Probably not, it seems to me. Social beings that we are, we need the sense of belonging and mutual responsibility that our identification with family and then other groups facilitates. Evolution favors what promotes survival, and the us/them distinction promotes survival and greater security and social cohesion. Still, the other side of in-group bonding can be mistrust, condescension or even hatred of others. So we need to consciously socialize ourselves and our children to be more open to those who are different. Yes, we are initially most comfortable with people like us. In time, though, we can—and most of us do—learn through experience to be more open to differences, and even to find them fascinating.

This is the classic particularism-vs.-universalism paradox. Identifying with one's own family, and other groups in which we find ourselves, shows healthy self-image and confidence. Our culture understandably puts emphasis on things like school spirit, Black pride (and other varieties of ethnic solidarity), patriotism, and so on. Yet when this goes to extremes, which is not at all rare, it becomes bigotry ("Not only are we safe, but they are dangerous"). Members of minority groups commonly feel socially left out or even maliciously discriminated against. Yet to believe that your country (or religion, or gender, etc.) is good does not logically require that others are inferior. You can even believe, where religions and other belief systems are involved, that you have the best one while understanding that others feel the same about theirs.

Family being the ultimate example of in-group belonging and loyalty, biblical tradition turned to it as the perfect metaphor for the harmony humanity needs to move towards mutual toleration and peace. Though plainly and painfully aware of the multiplicity of peoples and nations, biblical tradition presents humankind as one family. At the beginning of Genesis God creates one human couple from whom all others descend. Ergo: one human family. When Adam and Eve beget two sons, Cain and Abel, the stage is set for a mythic first human quarrel. When Cain becomes jealous of his brother, God warns Cain that he needs to calm down; he can control himself, "master" his urge to (violent) sin (Gen 4:7). But Cain goes ahead and kills Abel, and when God confronts him responds with the rhetorical question, "[A]m I my brother's keeper?" (Gen 4:9). Cain may have thought the answer should be "no," but in the context of the story and the punishment which follows, the lesson of Genesis is that we are, indeed, responsible for our siblings.

We could look at any one of a series of brother stories; very significantly, in these early tales of Genesis the brothers are identified as the progenitors of different peoples around what was for our ancestors the whole world. That is, Isaac and Ishmael are both sons of Abraham, and Jacob and Esau are both sons of Isaac. They came to be known as fathers of different peoples, but there was never any doubt in antiquity or today that they were, and are, kin. When Jacob, having run for his life after defrauding Esau of his birthright, returns home years later, he worries that Esau will still want to kill him. When he sees his brother approaching with four hundred men, he fears a slaughter. He splits his camp in two so that at least half of them can escape if there is about to be a slaughter. But Esau and Jacob have both matured. They embrace. Jacob offers his brother gifts, and Esau says he doesn't need anything, for God has already blessed him abundantly. "But Jacob said, 'No, I pray you; if you would do me this favor, accept this gift; for to see your face is like seeing the face of God!" (Gen 33:10) As family, despite our quarrels and rivalries, we can represent God to one another—but first we must set aside grievances and reconcile.

Nor does this apply only to Hebrews and their immediate brothers. Earlier in Genesis the daughters of Abraham's brother Lot, mistakenly thinking they and their old father are the last people left alive in the world when Sodom and Gomorrah are destroyed, have sexual relations with Lot while he is too drunk to know what is going on. They believe they are acting to save humankind from extinction, which to my modern ears sounds noble (Gen 19:23–38). But the biblical authors' horror at incest is being put to a different use in this story. The women become pregnant with sons named Ammon and Moab, which is to say they are the progenitors of two of Israel's traditional enemies. The implicit question being answered is how Ammonites and Moabites can be such awful people. They are children of incest! Yet here, even though there is no reconciliation in the tale, the secondary lesson is plain: even enemies are direct relatives! The chapters of "begats," Genesis 10 and 11, which Bible classes tend to skip over, must likewise have demonstrated to the biblical audience that the whole world is kin. Close relatives and distant cousins, all are part of one human family.

The idea of one human family is not mere wishful thinking or hyperbole. As a matter of science as well as religion, *Homo sapiens* has evolved from common ancestors,[18] and when we find common elements of human nature arising naturally from our evolved bodies and especially brains, that further demonstrates that we are, in many ways, related to one another. Yearning for world peace, some have worked to minimize differences among the various

18. See "Mitochondrial Eve" at Wikipedia.com.

branches of the family. All should give up their inherited languages and learn Esperanto, for example, or all religions should forget their differences and accept some one of them (Bahai makes that a particular goal, but seemingly with no more success than can be claimed by the missionaries of other faiths). Such efforts, in any given case either well-intentioned or arrogant and ethnocentric, are understandable, but actually miss the main biblical point: we need not be alike; we need only learn to respect our differences. Family members are related, but not identical. We can each develop, take on new interests, even move to other nations or convert to other religions. But we never lose our own background, our own story, which lies at the root of the identity we develop over the years.

Nobel laureate Elie Wiesel, encountering a young Jew who reported wanting to leave his particular Jewish identity behind and identify, instead, with all humanity, responded pungently:

> . . . the Jew influences his environment, though he resists assimilation. Others will benefit from his experience to the degree that it is and remains unique. Only by accepting his Jewishness can he attain universality. The Jew who repudiates himself, claiming to do so for the sake of humanity, will inevitably repudiate humanity in the end. A lie cannot be a stepping stone to truth, it can only be an obstacle.[19]

This could apply as well to any group. Furthermore, our various particular identities have deep emotional resonance—love of one's family, community, nation, faith group, and so on, and often their culture and history. There are many facets to individual identity, which is to say, by way of example, that I am male, Jewish, American, a clergyperson and a folk- and classical-music lover. It is alright if I get choked up while singing an American patriotic song one day and while gazing out from the Mount of Olives over Jerusalem another. These and many other aspects of what I feel as my story are valid and important parts of both my uniqueness and my humanity. "I am large, I contain multitudes," exclaimed Walt Whitman.[20] We share human nature and the same small planet, which is quite a lot. So we should be sufficiently self-aware and self-critical to overcome inherited prejudices without demanding self-denial of ourselves or others.

19. Wiesel, "To a Young Jew Today," 172–73.
20. Whitman, "Song of Myself," 96.

BACK TO THE LINEAR

Great is peace, for peace is to the world as leaven is to dough.

—PEREK HaSHALOM 1:1[21]

When the Holy One, blessed be He, created the first man, He took him and led him round all the trees of the Garden of Eden, and said to him, "Behold My works, how beautiful and commendable they are! All that I have created, for your sake I created it. Pay heed that you do not corrupt and destroy My universe; for if you corrupt and destroy My universe; there is no one to repair it after you.

—*MIDRASH RABBAH, ECCLESIASTES RABBAH, 7:13*

Very well, then, we are hardwired to need others, but also to pursue selfish interests—which at the extremes explains all sorts of sociopathic behavior from lying and theft to threats, violence and even murder. We are also hardwired to love, cooperate and to be empathetic. We learn that law and morality are generally in our self-interest, but we remain subject to temptation, sometimes (and for some habitually) violating norms if we think we can get away with it. Over the ages we have organized into small clans and then larger and larger groups to work together and minimize antisocial behavior. We have moved on to larger and larger societies, states and alliances of states, for as size and power accumulate so does the temptation to exploit smaller or otherwise weaker groups—conquest, blackmail, colonialism. Yet within these larger groups sharing of identity and culture leads to a sense of mutual responsibility and loyalty. We organize police, courts and jails, and armies needed for defense even when not intended for conquest. For centuries government power has enhanced the rule of law and dramatically reduced violent deaths.[22] Thus in society as well as in our individual brains there are mechanisms for cooperation as well as for selfish gain. What I like to call the balance of the selfish and the selfless is actually weighted towards the selfless, generous and cooperative side. We each do better in an orderly and safe environment.

I need hardly add that we are far from doing away with crime within societies or war and the threat of war between them. Our biblical ancestors intuited human unity even in a world full of petty warlords and brutal empires. Morality, education and other civilizing influences have continued to

21. *Perek HaShalom*, 59a.
22. Pinker, *Better Angels of Our Nature*, 59–128.

develop. Yet after the twentieth century's world wars and genocidal atroci-
ties—the Holocaust, Stalin's slaughters in the Soviet Union, the "killing
fields" of Cambodia, starvation in Biafra, etc.—many moderns despair of
biblical and other utopian dreams of world peace. Even with these modern nightmares, however, Harvard's Steven Pinker provides voluminous
evidence of progress against violence over the ages in his 2011 book, *The
Better Angels of Our Nature: Why Violence Has Declined*. We are not utterly
depraved. But neither should we expect a utopian era around the corner.

Growing worldwide economic interdependence, increased understanding and communication fostered by the computer revolution and no
doubt many other factors have inhibited worldwide conflicts à la World War
II for many decades. In addition, a large part of the reason for such peace as
we enjoy probably arises from the catastrophic potential of nuclear weapons.
Thermonuclear war is almost too horrific to contemplate. A worldwide nuclear conflagration could kill millions or even billions and, with dust clouds
and radioactive fallout, could quite possibly make the planet uninhabitable.

Even if we continue to avoid nuclear catastrophe, many fear that global
warming and other man-made environmental dangers threaten humanity's
survival unless we can rally unprecedented multinational cooperation to
address them. As the UN's Intergovernmental Panel on Climate Change was
about to release an extensive report on the urgent need to address climate
change, two experts in the field contributed an opinion piece to the *New
York Times* explaining that global warming is already so serious that successfully halting it is difficult to imagine. "The world would need to reduce
greenhouse gas emissions faster than has ever been achieved, and do it ev-
erywhere, for 50 years." The article was titled "Stopping Climate Change
Is Hopeless. Let's Do It." Humankind, they argued, has successfully faced
"seemingly insurmountable" challenges in the past. Beyond reason alone,
the scientists appeal for religious-style fervor and idealism, faith that we can
do more than we have ever done before. "The rewards of solving climate
change are so compelling, so nurturing and so natural a piece of the human
soul that we can't help but do it."[23]

We have always had problems, and always found ways to cope. How
have we not given up when new, monumental threats—world-conquering
armies, the Black Death, or climate change—have arisen? The challenge is
magnified but not fundamentally changed in our epoch, when joint effort
may be our only hope. Simply setting out the known facts for all to consider,
a secular approach, is vital. But we need something more: the fervor which
religion might inspire. To move forward (the linear, Western religious

23. Schendler and Jones, "Stopping Climate Change."

vision) we need faith—which, the reader should recall, starts with what we can know empirically, but then dares to go beyond the evidence without contradicting it. The existential predicament and the religious dream remain unchanged. Messianism may never culminate in utopia, but humanity has made measurable progress and can make more: that is our mission beyond survival alone.

Where did religious people get this messianic vision? Personal-God-concept answer: God revealed it. Philosophical-God-concept answer: in awe of the wondrous natural order and its moral implications, and yearning for better, more harmonious, righteous living, we figured it out, dreamed and envisioned it. Then, in our various scriptures, we expressed the conviction that we are one human family. The mythic notion that history began with divine creation may have originated simply for lack of a better answer. But the image of history as a line implies an end, not only a beginning. Envisioning a positive end time was a natural way to imagine the yearned-for harmony among people and peoples—and between people and the rest of creation too.

Secularists are more than welcome to share these convictions. But what will they base them on if not a sense of *mitzvah*, of commandedness and obligation, as subjects of God or divine order? From reason and science alone? Some will. But how interested are most people in deriving their values by rigorous reasoning? Most are more likely to get the message in religious community, hearing Scripture and praying regularly "to perfect the world under the sovereignty of God," as Jews pray,[24] or "The Lord's Prayer" ("Thy kingdom come, Thy will be done, On earth as it is in heaven"; Matt 6:10), a staple of Christian prayer. With reasonable frequency so as to reinforce values, will more people pray and learn together, or study philosophy, psychology, political science or other disciplines? We may try any or all of these. Religion, science and disciplined thinking of all sorts share the desire for truth. The goals of survival and, in the process, of peace lend meaning to our corporate as well as individual existence. Whatever any individual can do to bring us closer to the messianic goal, moreover, including adding to the store of other divine intangibles—not only of peace, love and harmony—advances the quest. Religions, fortunately, are organized to build and motivate idealistic communal as well as individual action.

Messianism, then, survives quite nicely with a philosophical rather than a personal theology. It is not science, but a faith step out beyond science. Religion and science at their best complement one another. From both

24. In *Aleinu* rubric in nearly every Jewish worship service, and the source of the *tikun olam* metaphor for "perfecting the world."

we know where we need to go if humankind is to survive. There is purpose in a religious world. There is only random drift in a purely scientific or secular one. *Religion and science concur that there is an order of being. Why call it God? Three reasons:*

1. *Because they are the same. The philosophical God is the personal God without the perceptual bias that leads us to mistakenly regard it as person-like.*

2. *He, she, it; father, king, creator; rock, order, process: all terms for the Divine are metaphors for a reality within existence that we cannot fully understand. God as order of being is suggested by science (no one doubts that order is real). At least as importantly, the divine intangibles (justice, love, truth, compassion, etc., etc.) suggested by our experience, like the order in which they and we are included, fill us with wonder and provide meaning to our living.*

3. *From long usage the term "God" bespeaks an attitude: the world, and our struggles within it, have purpose and meaning. They, and we, can achieve holiness.*

Bibliography

Abrams, M. H., ed. "Kubla Khan." In *The Norton Anthology of English Literature*, 2:197–199. New York: Norton, 1962.

Aleichem, Sholem (penname Sholem Rabinovich). *Tevye the Dairyman and Motl the Cantor's Son*. Translated by Aliza Shevrin. New York: Penguin, 2009. The original Yiddish Tevye stories appeared from 1894 to 1916.

Alter, Robert. *The Art of Biblical Poetry*. New York: Basic Books, 1985.

Brandt, Anthony, and David Eagleman. *The Runaway Species: How Human Creativity Remakes the World*. New York: Catapult, 2017.

Borowitz, Eugene. *A Laymen's Introduction to Religious Existentialism*. New York: Delta, 1965.

Buber, Martin. *I and Thou*. Translated by Ronald Gregor Smith. 2nd ed. New York: Scribner's, 1962.

Cahill, Thomas. *The Gifts of the Jews: How a Tribe of Desert Nomads Changed the Way Everyone Thinks and Feels*. New York: Anchor/Nan A. Talese, 1999.

Carroll, Sean. *The Big Picture: On the Origins of Life, Meaning, and the Universe Itself*. New York: Dutton, 2016.

Churchland, Patricia. *Braintrust: What Neuroscience Tells Us about Morality*. Princeton, NJ: Princeton University Press, 2011.

Cox, Harvey. *The Secular City*. Rev. ed. New York: Macmillan, 1965.

Damasio, Antonio. *Descartes' Error: Emotion, Reason, and the Human Brain*. New York: Grosset/Putnam, 1994.

———. *The Feeling of What Happens: Body and Emotion in the Making of Consciousness*. Orlando: Harcourt, 1999.

———. *Self Comes to Mind, Constructing the Conscious Brain*. New York: Pantheon, 2010.

———. *The Strange Order of Things: Life, Feeling, and the Making of Cultures*. New York: Pantheon, 2018.

Dennett, Daniel. *Darwin's Dangerous Idea: Evolution and the Meaning of Life*. New York: Simon & Schuster, 1995.

————. *From Bacteria to Bach and Back: The Evolution of Minds*. New York: Norton, 2017.

————. *Kinds of Minds: Towards an Understanding of Consciousness*. New York: Basic Books, 1996.

Dillard, Annie. *Pilgrim at Tinker Creek*. New York: Perennial Library, 1985 (first edition 1974).

Dostoevsky, Fyodor *The Brothers Karamazov*. Translated by Constance Garnett. New York: Modern Library/Random House, n.d. Russian original version published 1880.

Dunbar, Robin. *How Many Friends Does One Person Need?: Dunbar's Number and Other Evolutionary Quirks*. Cambridge, MA: Harvard University Press, 2010.

Eagleman, David. *Incognito: The Secret Lives of the Brain*. New York: Pantheon, 2011.

Emerson, Ralph Waldo. "Self-Reliance." In *The Essential Writings of Ralph Waldo Emerson*, 132–53. Paperback ed. New York: Random House, 2000. First edition of essay published 1841.

Fletcher, Joseph. *Situational Ethics: The New Morality*. Louisville: John Knox, 1966.

Freedman, H., and Maurice Simon, eds. *Midrash Rabbah*. 10 vols. Vol. 1, *Genesis Rabbah*, translated by H. Freedman. Vol. 3, *Exodus Rabbah*, translated by H. Freedman. Vol. 8, *Ecclesiastes Rabbah*, translated by L. Rabinowitz. Vol. 9, *Song of Songs Rabbah*, translated by Maurice Simon. London: Soncino, 1939.

Freud, Sigmund. *The Interpretation of Dreams* (1900). Standard Edition of the Complete Psychological Works of Sigmund Freud. Translated by James Strachey. See http://www.freudquotes.blogspot.com/2016/10/the-interpretation-of-dreams-is-royal.html.

Frymer-Kensky, Tikva. *In the Wake of the Goddesses: Women, Culture, and the Biblical Transformation of Pagan Myth*. New York: Free Press, 1992.

Galernter, David. *The Tides of Mind: Uncovering the Spectrum of Consciousness*. New York: Norton, 2016.

Gates of Prayer, the New Union Prayer Book. New York: Central Conference of American Rabbis, 1975.

Gazzaniga, Michael. *Human: The Science Behind What Makes Us Unique*. New York: HarperCollins, 2008.

Gillman, Neil. *Sacred Fragments: Recovering Theology for the Modern Jew*. Philadelphia: Jewish Publication Society, 1990.

Gittlesohn, Roland B. "Mitzvah without Miracles." In *Gates of Mitzvah: A Guide to the Jewish Life Cycle*, edited by Simeon J. Maslin, 108–10. New York: Central Conference of American Rabbis, 1979.

Gladwell, Malcolm. *The Tipping Point: How Little Things Can Make a Big Difference*. New York: Little, Brown, 2000.

Graziano, Michael. *Consciousness and the Social Brain*. New York: Oxford University Press, 2013.

Greenberg, Irving. "Cloud of Smoke, Pillar of Fire: Judaism, Christianity, and Modernity after the Holocaust." In *Auschwitz: Beginning of a New Era?*, edited by Eva Fleischer, 7–55. New York: Ktav, 1977.

Ha'am, Ahad (penname Asher Ginzberg). "Shabbat and Zionism." *HaShiloach* 3/6 (1898). Hebrew original: benyehuda.org/read/2786.

Haidt, Jonathan. *The Happiness Hypothesis: Finding Modern Truth in Ancient Wisdom*. New York: Basic Books, 2006.

Hauser, Marc D. *Moral Minds: How Nature Designed Our Universal Sense of Right and Wrong.* New York: HarperCollins, 2006.

Hertz, Joeph H. *The Authorized Daily Prayer Book.* Rev. ed. New York: Bloch, 1948.

Heschel, Abraham Joshua. *The Prophets.* New York: Harper & Row, 1962.

Hoffman, Lawrence. *The Art of Public Prayer: Not for Clergy Only.* 2nd ed. Woodstock, VT: Skylight Paths, 1999.

Hopkins, Gerard Manley. *Poems and Prose of Gerard Manley Hopkins.* Baltimore: Penguin, 1953.

Isaacson, Walter. *Einstein: His Life and Universe.* New York: Simon & Schuster, 2007.

Jacobs, Louis. "Shavuot." In *Encyclopaedia Judaica,* 14:1319–22. Jerusalem: Keter, 1971.

Kahneman, Daniel. *Thinking, Fast and Slow.* New York: Farrar, Straus and Giroux, 2011.

Kaplan, Mordecai M. *Judaism as a Civilization: Toward a Reconstructionism of American-Jewish Life.* New York: Reconstructionist, 1957; first edition, New York: Macmillan, 1934.

———. *The Meaning of God in Modern Jewish Religion.* New York: Reconstructionist, 1962.

King, Martin Luther, Jr. "Remaining Awake Through a Great Revolution." Speech delivered at the National Cathedral, Washington, DC, March 31, 1968. Martin Luther King, Jr. Research and Education Institute, Stanford University, Stanford, CA. https://kinginstitute.stanford.edu/king-papers/publications/knock-midnight-inspiration-great-sermons-reverend-martin-luther-king-jr-10.

Klagsbrun, Francine, ed. *Voices of Wisdom: Jewish Ideals & Ethics for Everyday Living.* Boston: Godine, 1980.

Kohler, Kaufmann. *Jewish Theology: Systematically and Historically Considered.* New York: Macmillan, 1918.

Kugel, James L. *The Great Shift: Encountering God in Biblical Times.* New York: Houghton Mifflin Harcourt, 2017..

Levitan, Daniel J. *This Is Your Brain on Music: The Science of a Human Obsession.* New York: Dutton, 2006.

Lewis, Thomas, et al. *A General Theory of Love.* New York: Vintage, 2000.

Linden, David. *The Accidental Mind: How Brain Evolution Has Given Us Love, Memory, Dreams, and God.* Cambridge, MA: Belknap/Harvard, 2007.

Luhrmann. T. M. *When God Talks Back: Understanding the American Evangelical Relationship with God.* New York: Knopf, 2012.

Luhrmann, Tanya. "Is That God Talking?" *New York Times,* May 1, 2013.

Maimonides, Moses. *The Guide for the Perplexed.* Translated by M. Friedlander. New York: Dover, 1956.

McEntire, Mark. *A Chorus of Prophetic Voices: Introducing the Prophetic Literature of Ancient Israel.* Louisville: Westminster John Knox, 2015.

Meacham, Jon. *American Gospel: God, the Founding Fathers and the Making of a Nation.* New York: Random House, 2007.

Meyer, Michael. *Response to Modernity: A History of the Reform Movement in Judaism.* New York: Oxford University Press, 1988.

Mecklenburger, Ralph. *Our Religious Brains: What Cognitive Science Reveals about Belief, Morality, Community and Our Relationship with God.* Woodstock, VT: Jewish Lights/Skylight Paths, 2012.

Miller, Lisa et al. "Neural Correlates of Personalized Spiritual Experience." *Cerebral Cortex,* June 2019, 2331–38.

Mishkan T'filah. New York: Central Conference of American Rabbis, 2007.

Mitchell, E. K. "Prophecy (Christian)." In *Encyclopedia of Religion and Ethics*, edited by James Hastings, 10:382–84. New York: Scribner's, 1928. https://archive.org/details/encyclopaediaofr10hastuoft/page/382/mode/2up.

Moore, George Foot. *Judaism in the First Centuries of the Christian Era: The Age of the Tannaim*. Cambridge, MA: Harvard University Press, 1927.

Nelson, David W. *Judaism, Physics and God: Searching for Sacred Metaphors in a Post-Einstein World*. Woodstock, VT: Jewish Lights, 2005.

Neubauer, Raymond L. *Evolution and the Emergent Self: The Rise of Complexity and Behavioral Versatility in Nature*. New York: Columbia University Press, 2012.

Newberg, Andrew, and Eugene D'Aquili. *Why God Won't Go Away: Brain Science and the Biology of Belief*. New York: Ballentine, 2001.

Newberg, Andrew, and Mark Waldman. *Why We Believe What We Believe: Uncovering Our Biological Need for Meaning, Spirituality, and Truth*. New York: Free Press, 2006.

Perek HaShalom, Derekh Eretz Zutta (a minor tractate of the Babylonian Talmud, where *Perek HaShalom* follows chapter 10). 59a. New York: M'orot, 1961.

Pew Forum. "Religious Landscape Study." May 12, 2015. http://www.pewforum.org/religious-landscape-study.

Pinker, Steven. *The Better Angels of Our Nature: Why Violence Has Declined*. New York: Viking, 2011.

"The Pittsburgh Platform." In *Jews and Judaism in the United States: A Documentary History*, edited by Marc Lee Raphael, 203–5. New York: Behrman House, 1983. https://www.ccarnet.org/rabbinic-voice/platforms/article-declaration-principles/.

Pritchard, James. *The Ancient Near East: An Anthology of Texts and Pictures*. Translated by E. A. Speiser. Princeton, NJ: Princeton University Press, 1958.

Rabinowitz, Louis Isaac. "Prophets and Prophecy, in the Talmud." In *Encyclopedia Judaica*, 13:1175–76. Jerusalem: Keter, 1972.

Sandmel, Samuel. *The Hebrew Scriptures: An Introduction to Their Literature and Religious Ideas*. New York: Knopf, 1963.

Schendler, Auden, and Andrew P. Jones. "Stopping Climate Change Is Hopeless. Let's Do It." *New York Times*, October 7, 2018.

Shakespeare, William. *King Lear*. In *The Complete Works of William Shakespeare*. Online publication, http://shakespeare.mit.edu/index.html.

Sharot, Tali. *The Optimism Bias: A Tour of the Irrationally Positive Brain*. New York: Pantheon, 2011.

Sheppard, Gerald T., and William E. Hebrechtsmeier. "Prophecy: An Overview." In *The Encyclopedia of Religion*, edited by Mircea Eliade, 12:11. New York: Macmillan, 1987.

Silver, Daniel Jeremy. "A Lover's Quarrel with the Mission of Israel." In *Contemporary Jewish Thought*, edited by Bernard Martin, 145–60. Chicago: Quadrangle, 1968.

Stein, Joseph. *Fiddler on the Roof*. Based on stories by Sholom Aleichem. New York: Crown, 1964.

Stern, Chaim. "A Guide to the Services and Their Themes." In *Gates of Understanding: A Companion Volume to Shaarei Tefillah: Gates of Prayer*, edited by Lawrence A. Hoffman, 171–75. New York: Central Conference of American Rabbis, 1977.

Tharp, Louise Hall. "The Song That Wrote Itself." *American Heritage* 6.1 (December 1956). http://www.americanheritage.com/song-wrote-itself.

Thilly, Frank, and Ledger Wood. *A History of Western Philosophy*. New York: Holt, Reinhart and Winston, 1957.

Tillich, Paul. *Dynamics of Faith*. New York: Harper & Row, 1957.

Union Prayerbook. Cincinnati: CCAR, 1895.

Waal, Frans de. *The Age of Empathy: Nature's Lessons for a Kinder Society*. New York: Harmony, 2000.

———. *The Bonobo and the Atheist*. New York: Norton, 2013.

Waldman, Marilyn Robinson. "Nubuwah." In *The Encyclopedia of Religion*, edited by Mircea Eliade, 11:3. New York: Macmillan, 1987.

Wegner, Daniel, and Kurt Gray. *The Mind Club: Who Thinks, What Feels, and Why It Matters*. New York: Viking, 2016.

Whitman, Walt. "Song of Myself." In *Leaves of Grass*. New York: Signet Classic/New American Library, 1950. First edition published 1855.

Wiesel, Elie. "To a Young Jew of Today." In *One Generation After*, 163–75. New York: Random House, 1965.

Wilczek, Frank. *A Beautiful Question: Finding Nature's Deep Design*. New York: Penguin, 2015.

Wilson, Edward O. *The Meaning of Human Existence*. New York: Livelight, 2014.

Wolfson, Ron. *Relational Judaism: Using the Power of Relationships to Transform the Jewish Community*. Woodstock, VT: Jewish Lights, 2013.

Wordsworth, William. "Lines Composed a Few Miles above Tintern Abbey, on Revisiting the Banks of the Wye During a Tour. July 13, 1798." In *The Norton Anthology of English Literature*, edited by M. H. Abrams et al., 2:78–79. New York: Norton, 1962.